First World War
and Army of Occupation
War Diary
France, Belgium and Germany

27 DIVISION
Headquarters, Branches and Services
Commander Royal Artillery
17 November 1914 - 21 November 1915

WO95/2256/1

The Naval & Military Press Ltd
www.nmarchive.com
Published in association with The National Archives

Published by

The Naval & Military Press Ltd

Unit 10 Ridgewood Industrial Park,

Uckfield, East Sussex,

TN22 5QE England

Tel: +44 (0) 1825 749494

www.naval-military-press.com

www.nmarchive.com

This diary has been reprinted in facsimile from the original. Any imperfections are inevitably reproduced and the quality may fall short of modern type and cartographic standards.

© **Crown Copyright**
Images reproduced by permission of The National Archives, London, England, 2015.

Contents

Document type	Place/Title	Date From	Date To
Heading	WO95/2256/1		
Heading	B.E.F. France & Flander First Anzac Corps H.Q. Commanding Heavy Artillery. 1917 Oct To 1918 Apr.		
Heading	27th Division Divl Artillery C.R.A. Nov 1914-Nov 1915		
Heading	C.R.A. 27th Division November & December 1914		
War Diary	Winchester	17/11/1914	20/12/1914
War Diary	Southampton Havre	22/12/1914	23/12/1914
War Diary	Arques	26/12/1914	26/12/1914
Miscellaneous	Copied From Br. Gen. Stoke's Papers		
Heading	C.R.A. 27th Division January 1915		
War Diary	Arques	02/01/1915	06/01/1915
War Diary	Dickebusch	07/01/1915	26/01/1915
Miscellaneous	Report On The Gun Positions Of The 27th Division	16/01/1915	16/01/1915
Heading	Hd Qrs R.A. 27th Division 27.3.15 1/2-27/3/15		
War Diary		01/02/1915	27/03/1915
Miscellaneous	Central Registry		
Miscellaneous	2nd Army Headquarters		
Miscellaneous	G.X. 379		
Miscellaneous	Headquarters 27th Division	05/03/1915	05/03/1915
Miscellaneous	Headquarters, 5th. Corps	08/03/1915	08/03/1915
Miscellaneous	Headquarters, 27th Division.		
Operation(al) Order(s)	27th Division Operation Order No. 29 "B"		
Miscellaneous	A Form Messages And Signals		
Miscellaneous	Reference Map 1/20,000		
Map	A New Commd Trench		
Miscellaneous	Reference Operation Order No. 29 Of Today		
Operation(al) Order(s)	27th Divisional Artillery Operation Order No. 3	05/03/1915	05/03/1915
Heading	H D Qrs R.A. 27th Division Vol III 30.4.15		
War Diary	Reninghelst	01/04/1915	10/04/1915
War Diary	Potijze	11/04/1915	30/04/1915
Heading	27th Division Hd Qrs R.A. 27th Division Part Of Vol III For 29th April 1915		
Operation(al) Order(s)	27th Divisional Operation Order No. 45 Appendix 1	17/04/1915	17/04/1915
Operation(al) Order(s)	5th Corps Operation Order No 12 Appendix II	26/04/1915	26/04/1915
Heading	Hd Qrs R.A 27th Division Vol IV 1-31.5.15		
War Diary	Potijze	01/05/1915	03/05/1915
War Diary	(H15a)	04/05/1915	05/05/1915
War Diary	Ypres (H15A)	06/05/1915	08/05/1915
War Diary	Ypres	10/05/1915	31/05/1915
Miscellaneous	G.O.C. Royal Artillery, 27th Division	27/05/1915	27/05/1915
Heading	27th Division Hd Qrs R.A. 27th Division Vol V 1-27.6.15 27th Division		
War Diary	Croix Du Bac	01/06/1915	14/06/1915
War Diary	Armentieres	15/06/1915	27/06/1915
Miscellaneous	Appendix I		
Miscellaneous	Appendix II		
Heading	27th Division Hd Qrs R.A. 27th Division Vol VI July 15		
War Diary	Croix-du-Bac	15/07/1915	31/07/1915

Heading	27th Division Hd Qrs R.A. 27th Division Vol VII August 1-Sep 1-15		
War Diary	Croix Du Bac	02/08/1915	16/09/1915
War Diary	Merris	17/09/1915	21/09/1915
War Diary	Mericourt	22/09/1915	30/09/1915
Miscellaneous	27th Divisional Artillery. Programme Of Operation Appendix I		
Miscellaneous	27th Divisional Artillery. Programme Of Operation Appendix II		
Miscellaneous	27th Divisional Artillery. Programme Of Operation Appendix III		
Heading	C.R.A. 27th Divn Oct 15 Vol VIII		
War Diary	Mericourt	01/10/1915	26/10/1915
Heading	26 Q. R.A. 27th Div. Nov 1915 Vol IX		
War Diary	Guinemicourt	21/11/1915	21/11/1915

WO 95/2256/1

B.E.F. FRANCE & FLANDERS

FIRST ANZAC CORPS. H.Q.

COMMANDING HEAVY
      ARTILLERY.
1917 OCT TO 1918 APR.

994

27TH DIVISION
DIVL ARTILLERY

C. R. A.

~~Nov~~ DEC 1914 – NOV 1915

C. R. A. 27th DIVISION

NOVEMBER & DECEMBER

1 9 1 4

27th Divisional Artillery

Army Form C. 2118.

WAR DIARY
-or-
INTELLIGENCE SUMMARY.
(Erase heading not required.)

Instructions regarding War Diaries and Intelligence Summaries are contained in F.S. Regs., Part II and the Staff Manual respectively. Title pages will be prepared in manuscript.

Hour, Date, Place	Summary of Events and Information	Remarks and references to Appendices
1914 Nov 17th WINCHESTER	Brig Genl A. Stokes D.S.O. assumed command of the Artillery of the 27th Division. Major R H Hare M.V.O. D.S.O. Royal Artillery took up his appointment as Brigade Major Artillery. W.O. Telegram #421 A.G. 4 #4460 A.G.4.	
Nov 19th immediate	The following units began to arrive: 95th, 96th(a), 98th(b), 99th(c), 18th(c) (b) 20th (a) 19th Batteries comprising (a) 19th (b) 20th (c) 3rd (d) 17th Brigades.	
Nov 20th "	Command having the 19th Brigade R.F.A. The 100th (20 Bde) 103rd Batteries arrive.	

Nov 25th "	The following extract from Dvl orders of this date shows the re-organization of Brigades & Batteries to form the Artillery of this Division.
	(a) The left half of 95th Battery will now form the 131st Battery
	      " 96th " " " 132nd "
	      " 98th " " " 133rd "
	      " 99th " " " 364th "
	      " 100th " " " 67th "
	(b) The 27th Div" Artillery will be organized as follows :-
	    1st Brigade 98th, 132nd, 133rd Batteries
	    19th " 95th, 96th, 131st "
	    20th " 67th, 99th(?), 364th "	

Army Form C. 2118.

WAR DIARY
INTELLIGENCE SUMMARY.
(Erase heading not required.)

Instructions regarding War Diaries and Intelligence Summaries are contained in F.S. Regs., Part II and the Staff Manual respectively. Title pages will be prepared in manuscript.

Hour, Date, Place	Summary of Events and Information	Remarks and references to Appendices
1914. Nov. 27th WINCHESTER	Completed horsing the Artillery of 27th Divn. with 1188 horses. The Bde Ammn Columns await personnel before drawing horses.	
Nov 30th	9 guns 9 limbers & 3 telephone wagons arrive for completing the 3 batteries of each Brigade to 4 guns each	
Dec 1st	Capt. J.B. Orde R.F.A. 98th Battery confirmed in his appointment as Staff Capt. R.A. 27th Divn. W.O. Telegram 4813 A.G.4.	
Dec 3rd Dec 11th Dec 12th	Lt Col H.B. Smiley assumes command of 1st Brigade 25 D.J Stevens R.F.A. Goins as A.D.C. to 9.0.0 27th Divn Arty. G.O.C. 27th Divn Arty and the Brigade Majors visit the 27th Divn Ammn Column	
Dec 14th	The Division carries out a route March in the neighbourhood of WINCHESTER.	
Dec 16th Dec 17th	The 27th Divn to be inspected by H.M. The King The following Divl. Order No 1 of 17th inst. is issued. Before leaving WINCHESTER yesterday 16th inst: H.M. The King graciously expressed to the Major General Comdg. The Divn his entire satisfaction with the appearance of the troops & their steadiness on parade. The first turn out of all ranks was the subject of comment and the trouble expended in the turn out & grooming of the horses of the R.F. Artillery did not escape notice.	

Army Form C. 2118.

WAR DIARY
-of-
INTELLIGENCE SUMMARY.
(Erase heading not required.)

Instructions regarding War Diaries and Intelligence Summaries are contained in F.S. Regs., Part II and the Staff Manual respectively. Title pages will be prepared in manuscript.

Hour, Date, Place	Summary of Events and Information	Remarks and references to Appendices
Dec 17th 1914 WINCHESTER	A farewell message from H.M. The King of 16th Dec. was read	
Dec 19th	The 19th Bde R.F.A. & 67th Battery with 81st & 82nd Inf. Bdes leave MAGDALEN HILL CAMP, WINCHESTER by march route to SOUTHAMPTON there to embark.	
Dec 20th	H.Q. 27th Div. Artillery with the remainder of 20th Bde & the 1st Bde R.F.A. accompanied by 80th Inf. Bde leave Camp at WINCHESTER by march route for SOUTHAMPTON there to embark. H.Q. Div. Arty. embarks with 4th R.B.	
SOUTHAMPTON	on S.S. AUSTRALIND and	
HAVRE Dec 22nd	Disembarked at HAVRE at 4 p.m.	
Dec 23rd	Lt. D. f Stevens proceeds in command of Div. Arty. H.Qrs. by rail to AIRE. Brig. Genl Stokes & Lt. Col Hale proceed by motor to ABBEVILLE, ST OMER & ARQUES.	
ARQUES Dec 26th	The following is the distribution of the Artillery of this Division which today is concentrated in the following areas:	
	80th Inf. Bde. Area — 20th Bde R.F.A. H.Qrs near SERRUS Div. Amm" Column WITTE	

(73989) W.4141—463. 400,000. 9/14. H.&J.Ltd. Forms/C. 2118/10.

WAR DIARY
INTELLIGENCE SUMMARY

Place: ARQUES

Date: Dec 26th

81st Inf/Bde Area — 1st Bde RFA near Boeseghem
82nd " " — 2nd A/Bg HQrs in Arques
19th Bde RFA in Renescure
GOC proceeded with POC Division to reconnoitre a line of defence from Renescure to Thiennes.

4

Army Form C. 2118.

WAR DIARY
or
INTELLIGENCE SUMMARY.
(Erase heading not required.)

Instructions regarding War Diaries and Intelligence Summaries are contained in F.S. Regs., Part II. and the Staff Manual respectively. Title pages will be prepared in manuscript.

Hour, Date, Place	Summary of Events and Information	Remarks and references to Appendices
ARQUES. Dec 26th to 1.9 am.	81st Inf Bde Area. — 1st Bde R.F.A near BOESEGHEM. 82nd Inf Bde Area — Div'l Arty H.Q" in ARQUES 19th Bde R.F.A. in RENESCURE G.O.C. proceeded with G.O.C. Div'l to reconnoitre a line of defence from RENESCURE to THIENNES.	

Copied from Br.- GEN. STOKE'S PAPERS.

RECOLLECTIONS OF YPRES 1915.

1st Brigade R.F.A. - Lt.-Colonel W.B. Emery, R.F.A.

Commanding.

---

1. The Brigade consisted of

    H.Q., 98th, 132nd and 133rd Batteries,
    Brigade Ammunition Column.

Went into action East of YPRES on Easter Monday, 5th April 1915. The 11th Battery joined the Brigade on the 8th April.

POSITIONS. Brigade H.Q. in Farm ½ mile N.E. of BELLEWAARDE Farm.

98th and 133rd Batteries in the east edges of a small wood 300 yards North of Brigade H.Q.

132nd Battery in echelon in a wood N. of BELLEWAARDE Pond.

The 11th Battery in Railway Wood.

The last-named battery was the only one which had any protection. Major Robertson immediately began to dig in his guns and detachments in the raised mound on which the wood stands, and made his position fairly proof against small shell.

The Brigade Zone originally covered the line HERENTHAGE - POLYGON WOOD. The wagon lines were about 1 mile west of POTIJZE south of the main road. Some German guns annoyed our Infantry near HERENTHAGE by enfilade fire which was extremely accurate and dangerous.

Two guns of 98th Battery were placed near WESTHOEK which enfiladed the opposing German Trenches so effectively that the German guns shut up.

Our Infantry lines of trenches remained in the same positions HERENTHAGE - POLYGON WOOD until ordered to retire to the G.H.Q. line on May 2nd/3rd.

On Sunday 18th April the Germans began to bombard the town of YPRES with very heavy shell.

On 20th April Germans used Tear Shell on our positions for the first time.

On the 22nd April the Germans attacked the French on our left and rear, and broke through to the Canal. At night the limbers were kept near the guns in case of accidents. The 148th Howitzer Battery had meanwhile been attached to the Brigade and was in action West of BELLEWAARDE Pond.

On the 23rd April the 133rd and 148th Batteries were turned round to fire North.

On the 24th the Germans attacked ST. JULIEN.

During the next few days there was heavy fighting about ST. JULIEN and a wood West of St. Julien.

My chief recollection of this time is the fact that the 148th Howitzer Battery had to shoot WEST, NORTH & EAST.

The 133rd faced WEST in the Western edge of their small wood; whilst the 98th Battery had a section shooting NORTH and another N.E. from the same wood.

The 132nd Battery alone continued to support our 27th Division Infantry.

The Wood, about 200 yards long by 100 yards broad in which the 133rd and 98th were, was shelled continuously, luckily by shrapnel which burst on the tree tops or were buried. The Batteries suffered very few casualties although not entrenched. The ground did not admit digging.

The Tear Shell were a nuisance.

The hollow in which the 148th was became full of fumes. Also the dug outs in RAILWAY WOOD became untenable.

Brigade H.Q. although in full view of the enemy and constantly shelled, from WEST, NORTH & EAST, was not actually hit.

Telephone Lines were perpetually being cut.

German aeroplanes were very in evidence, flying low and observing at leisure.

I saw one brought down by our Infantry Fire.

During this time one gun of 132nd in a wood absolutely enfilading the MENIN ROAD was most useful in preventing the Germans using that road.

On Monday 26th April the Lahore Division attempted to retake a wood west of ST. JULIEN but made no progress.

Fighting continued about the wood on the 27th and 28th during which time the Germans maintained a heavy fire from a large number of guns.

On the 29th April, the wagon lines were sent back to the West of YPRES near VLAMERTINGHE. They had suffered very heavy casualties.

On Friday 30th April I went to Division H.Q. and was instructed to withdraw to positions nearer YPRES facing north.

My Brigade H.Q. had meanwhile been moved to some dugouts in a Railway Cutting owing to communications with the Farm becoming impossible.

On 1st May one section per Battery was withdrawn to positions nearer Ypres; 98th in a hedge in the open just north of the Railway line about 1 mile east of Railway Crossing on MENIN ROAD, 132nd and 133rd North of MENIN Road opposite l'Ecole de Bienfaisance. The 11th Battery near the LILLE GATE E. of the Ramparts. On the night of the 1st/2nd the Germans kept up very heavy shell fire on all roads. Orders had been issued to carry out the retirement on this night, but were cancelled. This was a curious coincidence. A general retirement under such a fire would have entailed heavy losses.

On the night of the 2nd/3rd May the general retirement to the line roughly BELLEWAARDE Pond - VERLORENHOEK was carried out in absolute peace. The remaining sections were retired to new positions.

Soon after dawn on the 3rd May the Germans advanced

cautiously under heavy covering fire of artillery, until they came in contact with our new line. Brigade H.Q. remained in dugouts on the railway.

The New Line had the serious disadvantage from an artillery point of view, that the high ground WESTHOEK ridge was given up. Observation of fire became difficult. We had no aeroplanes co-operating.

The Germans were very successful in setting fire to farms with incendiary shell. Their shooting was extraordinarily accurate. Two or three shell sufficed to put a farm into a blaze. Fxx From our H.Q. we watched many farms set on fire.

On May 4th German shelling was very heavy and made our communications hopeless by telephone. Runners were the only possible method.

On 5th May Germans shelled our Infantry trenches all day. We had no means of stopping them as they were all under cover and observation was impossible.

Our Brigade fire was directed onto such enemy infantry as were visible.

Our Batteries were not spotted by the Germans until the 8th May when the area about 132nd and 133rd was very heavily shelled. Most of 133 guns were put out of action. 132 escaped punishment until a premature gave away their exact position, when they were quickly put out of action by extremely accurate fire from 5.9" howitzers, losing many of the detachments.

133 withdrew at dusk to a new position close to the Ramparts. 132 was withdrawn also.

On 10th May Germans shelled 3rd K.R.R's out of their trenches in HOOGE CHATEAU WOODS. They fell back to the rear of the Woods. 98th Battery was badly shelled. This battery did good work all day and greatly impeded the German advance down the Railway. Firing over the sights at about

1000 yards.

Major Stevenson was wounded. The Battery suffered many casualties and was withdrawn to rest, at dusk, being replaced temporarily by the 99th Battery.

I would here mention that the Brigade H.Q. was in front of the battery positions, being in a cutting, on the railway. On the 8th May Telephone lines were cut continually and the only means of conveying order to batteries was by sending officers. Eventually all other officers being away I had to go myself to the 122nd and 133rd Batteries to direct them onto the enemy's infantry who were making considerable progress, and I was thus an eyewitness of the sudden overwhelming of the 132nd Battery by a few well-directed salvoes of 5.9's.

On May 11th, owing to the impossibility of keeping telephonic communication up, H.Q. was moved to the East side of the Canal at KRUISSTRAAT. The railway dugouts being kept as an O.P. for use by day. On this day the 4th Durham Light Howitzer Battery of 5-in. Hows. came into action. Owing to their short range it was essential to put them forward and the only places that offered any cover was the same hedge in which the 98th Battery had suffered so badly; but they were able to fire from a point nearer the railway. As a matter of fact the Germans continued to shell the old 98th position but never found the 4th Durhams who did very good work.

On May 13th the 2nd Cavalry Division was fiercely attacked and fairly shelled out of their trenches from VERLORENHOEK to BELLEGARDE. The cavalry suffered severely but maintained their ground. General de Lisle sent me a very complimentary letter thanking the gunners for the support given.

I would mention that a section of 4.7-in guns was in action under my command at this time, but owing to their condition and bad ammunition I had to stop them from firing anywhere near our own line.

May 14th, 15th, 16th to 23rd were fairly quiet.

On 15th May I shewed Major Chapman of the 5th. Durham How. Battery round the position. Also Colonel Stockley ~~Comely~~ Commanding Durham Brigade.

May 17th. Finding Brigade H.Q. too far from the Batteries, it was moved into the Ramparts close to the Sally Port e. of Menin Gate, where it remained until we left Ypres.

Monday 24th May. The Germans attacked at 2.20 a.m. with gas and shell all along the line; and broke in between Hooge and the Railway.

They did not penetrate beyond the woods, and I think there is no doubt that their advance was held up mainly by the fire of the 1st Brigade R.F.A. Hooge Chateau was held throughout by a Cavalry detachment, but I have been informed by eye-witnesses that between that point and Bellwarde the Artillery fire practically prevented the enemy's advance far south of the Pond.

The Gas was very trying as we had only indifferent respirators.

My own Staff were nearly all more or less overcome. Personally I kept a wet silk handkerchief over my face as much as possible, smoked most of the day and suffered no ill effects. The batteries were firing hard all day. Lucklily they were well concealed and only a few guns were put out of action.

I remember one gun of 133rd Battery was hit by a 5.9 shell and only the gun itself was left intact, upside down on a very twisted trail.

As a matter of interest I recount the following episode.

About 3.30 p.m. I received a message by telephone ordering me to meet Br.-General X at the Lille Gate at 4 o'clock.

I could not gain any more information. I was at the Lille Gate at 4 o'clock and whilst waiting for the General wandered about and found infantry lying down in column along the Canal Bank. I could get no information from them as all the officers were away at a pow-wow. I tried to get through to the Div. H.Q. from a telephone centre just across the bridge with a view to finding out what was going on, but could not.

Eventually Br.-General X arrived about 6.30 p.m. and informed me that he had been ordered to make a counter attack on the Line HOOGE - BELLEWAARDE, in conjunction with another brigade, starting at 7 p.m. (I think) to turn the Germans out. He had been ordered to have his H.Q. at the Lille Gate. *I was acting CRA north of Ypres 27th*

Division at the time, and had lines out connecting me to the F.O.Os. and Infantry. There was no communication from the Lille Gate. My lines were mostly cut but still were better than nothing. It was a matter of difficulty to arrange connection with and support for a counter-attack at half hour's notice after a very hard day's fighting.

A line was laid by my telephonists to the Infantry Brigade H.Q. at Lille Gate. I managed to find an Officer to act as liaison with the Infantry attacking line. N.B. The officer was a last joined Subaltern from the Shop and had been in France about a week. The guns had been shooting at the point of attack all day, so presumably had the range fairly accurately. As a matter of fact, the two Infantry Brigades failed to make liaison, owing I believe to the severe losses sustained en route to the points of assembly. One Brigade went up the Railway which was an absolute death trap. Anyway I was able to maintain conversation with my F.O.O. throughout the night, and, happening to know the country well, to direct him by telephone where to go and what to do, and from his reports to judge the rate of fire required from time to time. He was able to tell me what was going on.

Unfortunately the counter-attack failed, owing I think to the darkness of the night which rendered any exercise of command impossible. I have always been convinced that if more time had been allowed for preparation of co-operation between the two Infantry Brigades and the guns, a counter-attack would have been successful.

In the 27th Division the liaison between guns and infantry was close, and we always know what the Infantry were doing and what they wanted us to do.

During this second battle of Ypres, on the other hand, as far as my experience went, we suffered from being left in complete ignorance of what Infantry were coming into our area, and what they were trying to do.

On several occasions, at dawn, I found a new Brigade or Division had arrived in the Salient which my Brigade was more or less covering, without any information having been vouchsafed as to their name, position of H.Q. or intentions. By the time I had managed to discover what they were doing it was generally too late to help them in any way.

Unfortunately they soon melted away under the German gun fire to which we could make no reply.

The supply of ammunition was ordinarily replenished by night. The only available route was through the town of Ypres and during the active bombardment, the Ammunition Column and Battery Wagons suffered many casualties.

Much credit was due to the personnel for their unfailing courage and energy. On some occasions it was necessary to replenish ammunition by day.

I cannot remember what the Brigade's casualties amounted to. Three Majors had to be replaced of whom 1 was wounded, 2 went sick. About 250 horses were killed.

The lack of heavy guns to deal with the German guns was a serious drawback. Our aeroplanes were conspicuous by their absence.

The Germans used large numbers of Balloons for observation which greatly annoyed us as we could not reach them.

The Brigade left Ypres on the night of the 30th-31st May for Armentieres and took over from the 24th Brigade on the night of the 31st May - 1st June.

(Sd) W.B.EMERY,
Br.-General.

C. R. A. 27th DIVISION

JANUARY 1915

Army Form C. 2118.

WAR DIARY
or
INTELLIGENCE SUMMARY.
(Erase heading not required.)

Instructions regarding War Diaries and Intelligence Summaries are contained in F. S. Regs., Part II. and the Staff Manual respectively. Title pages will be prepared in manuscript.

Place	Date	Hour	Summary of Events and Information	Remarks and references to Appendices
ARQUES	1915 Jan 2nd		Orders were sent to 13th, 19th & 20th Bdes last evening this morning with a view to carrying out a sudden move. This scheme was carried out today.	
	Jan 3rd		The Div'l Comm'l Col. is out today to carry out a sudden move with a view to practising them in turning out quickly.	
	Jan 4th		G.O.C. & staff proceed to DICKEBUSCH to inspect gun positions & to make arrangements with the staff of the 32nd French Div" for taking them over	
	Jan 5th		1st Bde R.F.A moving under orders of 50th Inf Bde billets at PRADELLES. G.O.C. R.A & staff with H.Q. 27 Div" move to BORRE	
	Jan 6th		1st Bde R.F.A moves to billets near DICKEBUSCH. 20th Bde R.F.A. moves under orders of 81st infantry Bongarts to a billetting	

(73989) W4141—463. 400,000. 9/14. H.&J.Ltd. Forms/C. 2118/10.

Army Form C. 2118.

WAR DIARY
or
INTELLIGENCE SUMMARY.
(Erase heading not required.)

Hour, Date, Place	Summary of Events and Information	Remarks and references to Appendices
Jan 6th	area between METEREN and BORRE, G.O.C. R.A. with staff move with 14.a. 27 Div. to BOESCHEPE. 15th Bde R.F.A. joins the Division – 4 guns 98th Battery 1st Brigade + 4 guns 11th Battery 15th Bde. replace a similar number of guns in positions E & S.E	
DICKEBUSCH Jan 7th	of DICKEBUSCH to cover So Wt Bde in trenches between the VIERSTRAAT – WYTSCHAETE road & ST. ELOI. Change made before dawn – Batteries registering all day. The 19th Bde of F.A moves today to PRADELLES with the 82nd Inf. Bde.	
Friday Jan 8th	The following in Installation of Artillery & congratulents today 1st Bde in action with 8 guns N.4.a. 15th Bde " " 10 guns N.4.C. 20th Bde " " 4 guns H.35.C. 13th How By getting into position N.10.a. 19th Bde in Infule near PRADELLES on the way to join the Division 116th Battery R.G.A Stth wit St.Ts.Br. 27th Div. A.O. m. G. 34 to N. 5.a 27th Amm Park on St. SYLVESTRE CAPPEL	Scale ¼₀₀₀ Revised ⁵⁹/ⁿᵒᵛ¹⁴ Belgium Sheet 28

Army Form C. 2118.

WAR DIARY
or
INTELLIGENCE SUMMARY.
(Erase heading not required.)

Hour, Date, Place	Summary of Events and Information	Remarks and references to Appendices
Wed: Jan 13th	The 27th Div: Ammn: Col: moves to billets in BOESCHEPE from RENINGHELST to make room for infantry nearer their trenches.	
Mon. Jan 19th	116th Heavy Battery arrives in the 27th Divisional Area to reoccupy a position about 1 Mile N.E. of DICKEBUSCH evacuated for it by the 48th Battery yesterday. H.A. is there. The 19th Bde F.A. moves up to DICKEBUSCH. The 20th Bde in action. The following is the system of visit filed in batteries - Every in action at onllen 15th Bde do do 19" & 20" B.A. relieve each other - Guns are not changed owing to the difficulty of getting them in & out of their positions.	
Tues: Jan 20th	The 116th Heavy Battery R.G.A. in position N.E. of DICKEBUSCH about 1 Mile.	
Sat: Jan 23rd	The 7th Battery R.F.A. moves to a position on the "bund" of the lake at DICKEBUSCH.	

Army Form C. 2118.

WAR DIARY
or
INTELLIGENCE SUMMARY.
(Erase heading not required.)

Instructions regarding War Diaries and Intelligence Summaries are contained in F.S. Regs., Part II. and the Staff Manual respectively. Title pages will be prepared in manuscript.

Place	Date	Hour	Summary of Events and Information	Remarks and references to Appendices

---

Army Form C. 2118.

WAR DIARY
or
INTELLIGENCE SUMMARY.
(Erase heading not required.)

Instructions regarding War Diaries and Intelligence Summaries are contained in F.S. Regs., Part II. and the Staff Manual respectively. Title pages will be prepared in manuscript.

Hour, Date, Place	Summary of Events and Information	Remarks and references to Appendices
Tues Jan 26th 1915	G.O.C R.A & Bde Major remained at DICKEBUSCH so as to be on the spot should the Germans decide to celebrate their Kaisers birthday by an attack	

RA/9
16/1/15

REPORT ON THE GUN POSITIONS OF THE 27th DIVISION.

The Batteries are placed as in the attached sketch.
The guns are well concealed and though hostile aeroplanes have been over them three or four times, they have not been located.

One Battery of the 20th Brigade occupying a former French position is very cramped but excellently ~~well~~ concealed, the guns being at less than ½ interval.

The zones are as in attached sketch.

No special ~~targets~~ tasks have been allotted to Batteries, the general principle being to register accurately the enemy's gun positions and entrenchments, fire to be opened on a vulnerable target, or in reply to hostile fire.

The O.C. the Infantry Brigade in the trenches is in communication with the Artillery Brigade Commanders.

With the exception of one Battery (Major White's) of the 20th Brigade, no extra expenditure beyond the amount laid down has taken place, Major White's Battery fired some 50 rounds today at what he considered a good target.

Of the 1st. and 15th. Brigades, one battery in each is kept in reserve, and the 19th. Brigade relieves ~~xxnd~~ the XXth.
No change of guns takes place only personnel. This is necessary owing to the heavy state of the ground.

The shelters are generally good. In some cases the detachments preferring them to billets. They and the roads are being improved daily.

The ~~lines~~ horses are all kept with the exception of a few for orderlies some distance in the rear.

The observing stations are as per sketch.

There have been breaks in the telephone communocations, but it appears to be improving daily.

The Heavy Battery is not yet in action, but application has

been made to the French to occupy a position near P in camp in
H. 29a. *They will be in action this morning.*

The G.O.C. R.A., 27th. Division is in communication with the Artillery Commanders and are cooperating with each other.

The XIXth. and XXth. Brigades from India have no Orderly Officer. All the English Brigades have. The Orderly Officer is very necessary.

In some Batteries there were a good many empty cases, they should not be allowed to accumulate in the Batteries.

The XVth. Brigade had some 50 rounds of H.E. Shell, of which about half has been expended.

The Howitzer Battery since its arrival had expended some 200 rounds.

The Ammunition Column and Park are all ~~are~~ full.

[signature]
Brigadier General R.A.
Vth. Army Corps.

Hazebrouck,
16/1/15.

121/5320

H.d Qrs. R.A. 27th Division

Vol II — 27.3.15

1/2 — 27/3/15

Army Form C. 2118.

WAR DIARY
or
INTELLIGENCE SUMMARY.
(Erase heading not required.)

Instructions regarding War Diaries and Intelligence Summaries are contained in F. S. Regs., Part II. and the Staff Manual respectively. Title pages will be prepared in manuscript.

Place	Date	Hour	Summary of Events and Information	Remarks and references to Appendices
	Mon Feb 1st 1915		99th Battery R.F.A. goes into a position East DICKEBUSCH & N.E of L'Etang de Dickebusch.	
	Tues. Feb 2nd 1915		364th Battery R.F.A in position about 1 mile N E of DICKEBUSCH. S of the BAILLEUL-YPRES road.	
	Fri Feb 5th 1915		Owing to a certain liveliness in the Section held by the 28th Division on our left, all batteries were harnessed & horses harnessed up last night from 9 pm until 6.45 am	
	Sat Feb 6th 1915		The same reason the same precautions were taken between 7.40 pm & 11.55 pm last night.	
	Mon. Feb 8th 1915		The 39th Battery 14th Bde joins the Division	
	Tues. Feb 9th 1915		This battery replaces the 52nd Battery 15th Bde whose Bde H.Q. has already left town to join the 4th Div.	
	Wed. Feb 10th 1915		The 80th Battery 15th Bde leaves its position - 2 guns 11th Battery are withdrawn and march to Div inspection 39th Battery withdrawn of Honsfoen(?) bit 11 A Battery - 80th Battery marches to join 5th Div.	
	Thurs Feb 11th 1915		Section D.A.C. also marches to rejoin 5th Bde.	

WAR DIARY
or
INTELLIGENCE SUMMARY

(Erase heading not required.)

Army Form C. 2118.

Hour, Date, Place	Summary of Events and Information	Remarks and references to Appendices
Sun. Feb 14th 1915	Germans having shelled Trenches E of ST ELOI this afternoon marked No 19, 20, 21, & 22 Vividly. Fire was opened at 4.5 pm & continued throughout the night until at 7am. the trenches having	
Mon. Feb 15th 1915	been reoccupied firing ceased – the following Ammn was expended 8 1" RBL 1591 rounds, 19 RBL 2231 rounds, 20th RBL 1952 rounds, 4.5" Hows 122 rounds. Total 5896 rounds – The following was received from the 82nd Bde who reoccupied Trenches Feb 15th 8.0 am "All trenches now reoccupied. My grateful G.R.J. for tremendous help"	
Fri. Feb 19th 1915	One new gun 4.7" replacing one of the two in 116th Battery which have been condemned is in action today. A second one is	
Sat Feb 20th 1915	way up from Railhead. A second new gun 4.7" of the 116th Battery is got into position	
Sun Feb 21st 1915	The 61st How Battery of 8th Bde arrives from 5th Divn & ordered to report to 3rd Divn: The 3rd How 116th Heavy Battery also goes into position –	
Mon Feb 22nd 1915	The 30th How Battery marches to report to 5th Divn =	
Tues Feb 23rd 1915	H.A. Battery R.F.A. numbered 14 E Battery Artillery 5th Corps.	

Army Form C. 2118.

WAR DIARY
or
INTELLIGENCE SUMMARY.
(Erase heading not required.)

Instructions regarding War Diaries and Intelligence Summaries are contained in F.S. Regs., Part II and the Staff Manual respectively. Title pages will be prepared in manuscript.

Hour, Date, Place	Summary of Events and Information	Remarks and references to Appendices
Thurs: Feb 25th 1915	During the explosion of a shell in the bore of a 4.7" gun 116th Battery killing 2 men & wounding 3 - the gun was put out of action - The 4th 4.7" gun is in position.	
Mon. March 1st Sat. Feb 27	General Sir H. Smith Dorrien wires "I have only just received the detailed report of the most ably planned & gallantly carried out successful counter attack made on morning of 15th instant under Brigadier General Longley & others and would like you to convey my thanks and congratulations to General Longley and Lieut Colonel Tuson who actually commanded the attack and all battalions who took part in it. Have also heard how splendidly the artillery supported the counter attack. Please convey to them my thanks. The South W. Res plans to capture the German trenches opposite	
Mon. Mar 1st Tues Mar 2nd	Our numbers 19 20 & 21 E of St Eloi; at 12.30 a.m. Tues Mar 2nd bombardment commences - other artillery - 6th Batteries 3 of each of 19th & 28th Btys - opens fire at that hour and continues firing until 3.0 a.m. when the infantry after having occupied 60 yards of the hostile trench - Numbers of wounded filed thro' BC 19 - with Bde were supposed under the orders of the	

10

WAR DIARY
or
INTELLIGENCE SUMMARY.
(Erase heading not required.)

Army Form C. 2118.

Hour, Date, Place	Summary of Events and Information	Remarks and references to Appendices
Tues Mar 2nd	Brig Genl Conway 80th Iny Bde whose troops were carrying it out. at 9.30 am the O.C 4/ K.R.R reports that the men were bombed out of the captured trench & fell back on their old trenches.	
Sat Mar 6th	A bombardment of the Enemy's Redoubts E of St ELOI has carried out today. - Our infantry have evacuated their trenches E & W of St ELOI shrapnel fire from their trenches E & W of St ELOI shrapnel fire from 6.35am was employed to keep hostile reinforcements from joining them until 12 noon when the bombardment in direction of the 6" How: 3rd Siege Battery. His 61st How Battery & the 116th Heavy Battery commenced. — Y Fire ceased at 5.30pm from 3rd Siege Battery. - Y at 6 pm from two others two. - The evacuated trenches were protected from two Germans by 15pdr shrapnel fire from 19th R 20th Batts R.F.A until the Infantry had reoccupied them. At 7.45pm - Numbers of rounds expended 18pdr 2337, 4.5", 137 4.7",105, 6".117.-	R.H Nave Lt Col B.M R.A 27th Div

WAR DIARY
or
INTELLIGENCE SUMMARY.
(Erase heading not required.)

Army Form C. 2118.

Hour, Date, Place	Summary of Events and Information	Remarks and references to Appendices
Tues Mar 9th 1915	The Enemys Redoubts S. & W. of ST ELOI were attacked by Artillery fire to day. The operations commenced at 7 am. Units employed 19 & 20 to Forts R.F.A. 61st Field Battery R.F.A. 116th Heavy Battery & 1 Section 2nd Siege Battery R.G.A. The Infantry Demonstrated at dawn the Redoubts opposite there &c that were being attacked. 15pdr Shrapnel was employed to prevent any hostile advance towards our supply Redoubts - All fire ceased 7.36 p.m. Rounds fired. 18pdr Shrapnel 310 do, 4.5" Howr: 111 Lyddite 16 Shrapnel 4.7" Guns 146 Lyddite 6" Howr. 136. The 6" Howr: 2nd Siege Battery left to rejoin 3rd Division.	
Wed March 10 1915	Carried out a programme of Artillery fire attacking a portion of our front.	
Thurs March 11 1915	Under orders from V Corps the Artillery of 27th & 28th Division attacked a hostile redoubt & Redoubts in O 3 c 8 5 (Map 1/40000 Belgium) - Batteries registered from 7.30 to 11.30 am.	

WAR DIARY or INTELLIGENCE SUMMARY

Army Form C. 2118.

Hour, Date, Place	Summary of Events and Information	Remarks and references to Appendices
Thurs. March 11th	Fire was opened in town wire at 2.30 p.m. & continued on parapets, worked trenches until 3.40 p.m. Observation from THE MOUND at ST ELOI – from Trench 23 c & from the Canal bank in I.33.d. – YPRES Batteries engaged 2 Batteries 20th Bde, 116th Heavy Battery R.G.A. 61st Hows. Battery R.F.A. on Hill adjoining works – 17th & 19th Battns on their own zones	
Fri. March 12th	Under orders V Corps the Artillery 27th Division with that of 28th Divn attacked HOLLANDSCHESCHUUR FARM. Cooperating with an attack by the III Division in the direction of WYTSCHAETE – Fire opened by 2 Batteries 1st Bde for wire cutting at 2.45 p.m. – at 3.20 p.m. Stand fast till 3.40 so as to synchronize with 3 rds.Bn's attack. Fire came at 4.20 p.m. This operation was delayed from 8 a.m. till 2.45 p.m. owing to mist. Batteries engaged.: I.A – 1st Bde – 2 – 19th Bde 61st Hows. Battery – 116th Battery on wire cutting targets approved in main. 2 – 20th Bde on their own zone	

WAR DIARY
or
INTELLIGENCE SUMMARY.
(Erase heading not required.)

Army Form C. 2118.

Hour, Date, Place	Summary of Events and Information	Remarks and references to Appendices
Sat Mar 13th	Bombarded HOLLANDSCHESCHUUR FARM in conjunction with 28th Divn & co-operating with 3rd Division.	
Sun. Mar 14th	Enemy open a very hot gun fire at 5.15 pm on ST ELOI & that N. of it. We lost trenches 1H to 20 and the MOUND – Guns opened fire at 5.20 pm on their zones round ST ELOI. Fire was kept up all night at varying rate of speed. The 1st, 19th & 26th Bdes were placed under orders of the Inf Brig adv. who was at VOORMEZEELE – All batteries of Brigade 27th Dn & the Arty. 28th Divn – to fire 3rd Division co-operated. Trenches East & close West of MOUND retaken by 7 am Mon Mar 15th one section 6" Howitzer Siege Battery arrived from 2nd Indian Divn at 6.30 am 15am 15th March	
Mon March 15th	Amm d Expended. 18 pdr 6810. 4.5" 140. 4.7" 427. From 8 am onwards abombardment of the MOUND & the enemys trenches was continued, the 28th Divn &	

WAR DIARY or INTELLIGENCE SUMMARY

Army Form C. 2118.

Hour, Date, Place	Summary of Events and Information	Remarks and references to Appendices
Mon Mar 15th	Co-operating - Firing ceased about 7pm. Ammn. expended 6/7pm 15pdr 18pdr 1637 4.5"244 4.7"232 6" How. 76.	
Tues Mar 16th	Shelled the MOUND at ST ELOI with 61st Battery and the 6" How. Battery. Swept up main Trench S. of ST ELOI with 1 section Bd. Sec. (6" How.)	
Sun Mar 21st	Orders rec'd. to relieve 1st Bde R.F.A. in action by 42nd Bde R.F.A. 3rd Divn. on night of Mar 21st – 22nd	
Mon Mar 22nd	28th Bde Heavy Artillery placed at disposal of 27th Divn. Coming from 6th Divn.	
Tues Mar 23rd	28th Heavy Brigade reaches ABEELE STA early this morning. The 11th & 132nd Batteries 1st Bde r 39th Battery 19th Bde on relief by 42nd R.F.A. – Marched from positions to billets by night t marched later with the 98th r 132nd Batteries into their new billets near ABEELE STA. The 98th r 133rd Batteries into their new billets near ABEELE STA. From position this evening at 8 pm all troops on 27th Divn. front came under orders B.G. O.C 3rd Divn.	
Wed Mar 24th	at 11.30 am. O.C R.a 3rd Divn. takes over command of the following artillery 27th (6th) Divn. now in position – 19th 5th two 39th Battery 20th Bde less 67th Battery – 61st How.Bty. 8th Bde 116th H. Battery and left section Bd. Siege Battery – H.Qrs. 27th Divn. Arty moves WRENINGHELST.	

WAR DIARY
or
INTELLIGENCE SUMMARY.
(Erase heading not required.)

Army Form C. 2118.

Hour, Date, Place	Summary of Events and Information	Remarks and references to Appendices
Thurs Mar 25th	67th Battery 20th Battn marched to Whet near POPERINGHE. Reliefs of 19th & 20th Batteries in action owned by 3rd Division takes place but sections withdrawn and subsequently ordered to be replaced in position & incoming batteries to rejoin 5th Divⁿ.	
Fri. Mar 26th.		
Sat. March 27th.	Lt. Colonel R.H. HARE M.V.O. D.S.O. handed over his duties as Brigade Major to Major V. ASSER D.S.O.	

27th Div. Artillery

Army Form A 2007.

CENTRAL REGISTRY.

Central Registry No. and Date.

Attached Files.

SECRET
9 L

SUBJECT, AND OFFICE OF ORIGIN.

Report on artillery operations
6th March 1915.

Referred to	Date 1915	Referred to	Date	Referred to	Date
G.X.379 from V Corps	9/3	Roberts			
				P.A.	Date

Schedule of Correspondence.

SECRET

2nd ARMY HEADQUARTERS.

No. 149

Time 8/25A   Date 9/3/15.

A.C. Very interesting Shaw

M.G., G.S.

G.

I.G.

D.A. & Q.M.G.

M.G., R.A.

M.G., R.E.

File.

Secret

V Corps
G.X. 379

2nd Army.

Reports on the Artillery Operations of the 5th March are forwarded herewith.

Very satisfactory results were obtained in front of trenches 19. 20. 21.

The results in front of trenches 16. 17. 18. were disappointing.

The operations - with some modifications - will be repeated tomorrow - 9th inst.

Hector Hunner
Comdg. 5th Corps

March 8th 1915

Secret

Headquarters,
    27th. Division.

G X 361

I beg to forward my report based on a short interview that I held to-night with Major Swayne, 116th. Battery R.F.A. and Lieut. Housden 61st. Battery, who were observing at the MOUND to-day for the 116th. Battery and the 3rd. Siege Battery respectively.

3rd. Siege Battery opened at 12 noon firing well over the enemy's forward trench with one gun. Ranges were altered in accordance with the observer's observations until he was able to report "last round fell between our trench and German". The next round (fired by No.2 gun it is believed) fell within 30 yards of the MOUND between it and the BREASTWORK knocking everyone in the neighbourhood down and fatally injuring a sergeant of the P.P.C.L.I. who was on the look-out. I shall make enquiry as to the shooting of this round and of some others which were somewhat erratic, and all it is believed from the same gun.

The fire was moved E. along the forward trench towards trench 22 where it is believed to have smashed the sap.

The observer then moved it West towards the MOUND which was approached as close as possible consistent with safety.

It is believed that the forward trench from the sap-head near trench 22 as far as the S in SAP on the accompanying plan was completely destroyed. Germans were observed to be blown up into the air. The saps leading up to this forward trench were also damaged.

2.   The 4.7" guns 116th. Battery did not satisfy Major Swayne as to their accuracy but he reports

that their fire did good execution on the enemy's main trench from in front of trench 17 to the front of trench 15.

According to Major Swayne the 61st. Battery put shell into the trenches of the forward trench opposite trenches 15 to 17 but were unfortunate in that many of their rounds fell between trenches and not into them.

March 6th. 1915.   Sd A. STOKES. Br. General.
                          G.O.C. R.A. 27th. Divisn.

P.S. Major Swayne is much indebted to Lieut. Torrens S.L.I. Brigade Machine Gun Officer for help of every kind while he was at the MOUND.

Headquarters
V*th* Corps

I have just received above and forward it at once. Probably we shall do more of the results after reconnaissance tonight and from the trenches in daylight.

I have noted Brig Gen Stokes' P.S. and shall bring note his name. All observers on the mound deserve the highest credit for observing in such an exposed position.

T.D'O. Snow
Maj Gen
Comg 27th Division

7/3/15

SECRET.

URGENT.

Headquarters,

    5th. Corps.

----

1.   In continuation of my G.S.468 dated 7th. instant on the subject of operation of 6th., the detailed report by G.O.C. R.A. has not yet reached me, but I trust to be able to forward it within the next few hours.

2. As regards effect of the fire there is little more to report, as the observing officers already quoted were in the best position to observe the effect.

I forward, however, copy, marked "A", of report by Brigadier General Commanding 80th. Infantry Brigade on the results as was apparent to the troops in the trenches the following morning.

3. There is no doubt the bombardment had excellent effect on the Left Section of the St ELOI Defences, that is about opposite trenches 20 and 21.

My opinion from the reports is that the front parallel has been much damaged and some parts destroyed. Probability the activity now displayed is from the main trench which it is hoped to destroy to-morrow.

The results opposite trenches 16, 17 and 18 were not as good as I had hoped but another effort will be made at same spot to-morrow.

The moral effect must also have been considerable on the enemy throughout the area bombarded, and our own infantry much appreciated the operation. It shewed them what our guns were capable of doing when ammunition was available.

I also attach, marked "B" a copy of Operation Order No.29 and a telegram amending this operation order, marked "C".

8th. March, 1915.　　　　　　　Major General.
　　　　　　　　　　　　　Commanding 27th. Division.

Since writing the above, I have received the report of the G.O.C. R.A. which I forward at once, marked "D". With regard to para 5 I have noted the names of Major O.R. SWAYNE R.G.A. and Lieut. E.J.T. HOUSDEN R.F.A. which have been brought forward by Brigadier General Stokes, on account of able work performed by them on this occasion at great risk to themselves.

"A"

Headquarters,
    27th Division.

As regards the bombardment of the enemy's trenches on 6th March, the Officer Commanding the Battalion holding the right of the line reports that the enemy's trenches in front of 15, 16, 17 and 18 trenches was not effective, as was only to be expected, since this portion was not really bombarded, hence the enemy is still working in the trenches and saps in front of and approaching the above trenches.

The Officer Commanding Left Battalion reports that he has little doubt but that a good deal of damage was done, as the enemy enemy were much quieter yesterday, and he appears to have ceased sapping.

The Officer in charge of 22 trench reported that good practice was made at the sap near old 21 trench, cries were heard from there, and a listening patrol sent out to this sap reported it unoccupied.

From 20 trench, on forenoon of 7th, parties were seen carrying planks along the OOSTAVERNE road near S.E. Corner of Square O 8 b whcih looked as though they were intended for repairs.

The Commander of trench 19 reported that the enemy's fire on his trench was not so accurate as usual, the inference being that the German rifle rests, which are usually set on the top layer of sandbags of our parapet had been destroyed ; but that when he left they appeared to be getting replaced.

8th March, 1915.   Sd. C.G.Fortescue,
                                             Br. General,
                                 Commanding 80th Infantry Brigade.

SECRET.   "B"   Copy No. 11.

27th Division Operation Order No. 29.

1. The enemy's Line of Defence immediately in front of our trenches 15 to 21, both inclusive, will be subjected to heavy artillery bombardment tomorrow, 6th instant, with the object of the total destruction of his trenches in this vicinity, and of communicating trenches leading up to them from his main line.

ARTILLERY.
2. The exact details of the artillery arrangements for the conduct of this operation, the guns to be employed and the ammunition to be expended has been arranged for by the G.O.C. R.A.

The first round of the actual bombardment will be fired at 12 noon.

The G.O.C. R.A. will arrange for additional observation officers to be ready at their posts to replace casualties, and for communication to be augmented.

3. (a) G.O.C. Left Section of Defence (80th Infantry Brigade) will arrange that immediately before daylight the garrison of trenches Nos. 15, 16, 17, 18 and 19 are temporarily withdrawn.

Directly it is sufficiently dark all the above mentioned trenches are to be re-occupied.

The garrison of trenches 19(a) and 20 will be reduced to half numbers before daylight on 6th instant, remainder to display more activity than usual.

At 11.45 a.m. these garrisons will be withdrawn temporarily to breastwork in rear, via communication trenches.

During this withdrawal shrapnel fire will be brought to bear on enemy's front at this point.

Trenches 19(a) and 20 will be re-occupied, via the communication trenches, directly the bombardment ceases.

The G.O.C. R.A. will arrange to inform Headquarters of the battalion concerned when this moment arrives.

Trenches 15 to 20, both inclusive, will, on reoccupation be at once repaired if damaged, their defences strengthened, and manned to be held permanently.

(b) Special vigilance is required to prevent any attempt by the enemy to advance and occupy our vacated trenches, by bringing to bear all possible rifle and machine gun fire. G.O.C. R.A. will be prepared to employ suitable artillery fire to prevent such action by the enemy.

4. Trenches in the Right Section of Defence will be strengthened during the 6th instant with a view to preventing any possible effort of the enemy to divert attention from the Left Section during the bombardment by attempting an attack on this portion of the Line.

G.O.C. R.A. will arrange that certain batteries are told off ready to divert fire so as to deal with such a contingency.

5. Arrangements will be made by G.O.C. Left Section (80th Infantry Brigade) in conjunction with C.R.E. for supplies of all R.E. Stores, obstacles, etc., being placed ready at hand in rear for repair of damaged trenches, and for strengthening of defence directly it is dark. A special carrying party (one company 9th Argyle and Sutherland Highlanders) is placed at disposal of G.O.C. Left Section of Defence until further orders.

The C.R.E. will detail suitable R.E. working parties to be ready to move forward with infantry on reoccupation of trenches.

6. During the bombardment the G.O.C. R.A. and G.O.C. Left Section of Defence (80th Infantry Brigade) will communicate direct.

7. Special attention is drawn to the necessity of all concerned adjusting watches to signal time.

8. Divisional Head Quarters (Report Centre) will be established at DICKEBUSCH from 11 a.m.

H I Reed
Lieut. Colonel, G.S.,
27th Division.

Issued at 5 10 p.m.

"A" Form.
Army Form C. 2121.

MESSAGES AND SIGNALS.

SECRET.

To ~~Issued on receipt (midnight 5/6th)~~ letter
By Addsssd (personally)

This message is on a/c of: "C"

TO: 80th Infantry Brigade.
G.O.C. R.A.

GOC 5 Corps to Maj Genl Snow Comdg 27 Divn

Sender's Number	Day of Month	In reply to Number	
G.R. 831	Sixth.		AAA

Reference Operation Order No. 29 of today
1. The G.O.C. R.A. will arrange to open fire ~~directly~~ directly after dawn 6th instant with 18 pdr shrapnel on the enemy's trenches in front of our trenches numbers 15, 16, 17 and 18.

This fire will continue until the bombardment at 12 noon commences.

It will be of such volume and at such a rate as G.O.C. R.A. considers sufficient to prevent any possibility of enemy occupying the above mentioned trenches which will be evacuated before dawn.

2. This fire is not to commence until G.O.C. Left Section (80th Inf. Bde) has reported to G.O.C. R.A. that these trenches are evacuated and clear of our troops. Arrangements must be made by G.O.C. Left Section to ensure rapid transmission of this information to G.O.C. R.A.

3. Acknowledge by wire.

Place: Twentyseventh Division.
Time: 12.50 a.m. 6.3.15.

Sd. H.L. Reed Lt. Col., G.S.,

P.T.O.

"A" Form.　　　　　　　　　　　　Army Form C. 2121.

MESSAGES AND SIGNALS.　　No of Message ____

The fire ordered in para one will be so directed
as long as the enemy makes no movement forward,
as to make him still imagine that trenches referred
to are still occupied i.e. with safety to imaginary
garrisons in their trenches.

Sd. H.L. REID. Lt. Col. G.S.

Secret

"D"

Reference Map. $\frac{1}{20,000}$.

Report on Artillery bombardment of Enemy's forward trenches in O 2 c and d and O 8 a by 27th Divisional Artillery on March 6th 1915.

1. Units employed:-

		Projectile
19th and 20th Brigades (each 3 batteries)R.F.A.		Shrapnel.
61st Howitzer Battery.R.F.A.	4.5"Howitzers.	Lyddite.
116th Heavy Battery.R.G.A.	4.7"Guns.	Lyddite.
1 Section 3rd Siege Battery	6" Howitzers	Lyddite (120 lb Shell)

2. The instructions and orders regarding it are contained in 27th Division Operation Order No.29 of 5th March.1915 and 27th Divisional Artillery Operation Order No.3 of same date.

The experiences of the day led to a modification of the original scheme.

3. Observing Stations were as follows:-

(i) At (a) THE MOUND O 2 d 2.8.

  (b) The BREASTWORK in O 2 d.

  (c) The R.B.Trench O 2 c.

  (d) The BRASSERIE N 6 a.

(ii) (a) is the principal O.S. From nowhere else can the enemy trenches E, S, and W of it be so well observed. It holds but 2 observers, one of whom observed for 3rd Siege Battery.R.F.A. and one for the 116th Battery.R.G.A.

The danger of disconnection due to hostile shell fire and the prime necessity of continuous communication once the infantry had vacated their trenches, for the purpose of the bombardment, necessitated duplicated lines of telephone wire.

(b) and (c) were each manned by 2 observers with duplicated telephones lines; the lines to (b) were cut by shell fire in at least 4 places as were the lines to (c) ; to (d) communication by 2 lines, though slow, was working all day.

(b) and (c) were designed to supplement the observation from the MOUND, (b) to the East and (c) to the West. It was found however, that (b) was too far down the reverse slope to permit of accurate observation in front of our trenches Nos. 19, 19a, 20 and 21 ; (c) affords a good view over all trenches from PICCADDILY FARM O 8 a 2.8 to the ST ELOI - WYTSCHAETE road.

(d) was used for observation for the 61st Battery and in the event of the failure of THE MOUND and R.B.Trench observation stations, could have observed the fire of the 6" Howitzer on the enemy trenches W.of ST ELOI.

Artillery Brigade Commanders and the Officers Commanding 61st Howitzer Battery, 116th Heavy Battery and 3rd Siege Battery were connected by telephone with their batteries and with Divisional Artillery Headquarters.

On the whole the communications which were mainly laid out and entirely supervised by Lieut: Goodwin.R.E. of the Divnl Signal Company, worked very well.

4. Programme.

The first modification in the orders regarding this bombardment, was conveyed in 27th Division Telegram G.R.831 (copy attached) directing fire to be opened at dawn with 18 pdrs.   In consequence of this

at 6.35 a.m one battery of 19th Brigade opened fire on the enemy opposite trenches 15 and 16, and one battery on the enemy opposite trenches 17 and 18.

at 7.a.m.   2 more batteries opened on the same targets at rates of fire ranging from 15 seconds to 1 minute *till* interval.

at 12 noon   the 6" Howitzers and 4.7" guns opened fire on their respective targets, the infantry in 19, 19a and 20 trenches having by this time evacuated them.

at 12.4 p.m 4.5" Howitzers also opened fire.

The 19th Brigade now ceased firing and the 20th Brigade was ordered to fire an occasional round opposite trenches 19, 19a, & 20.

In the meantime the enemy was shelling ST. ELOI & the adjacent trenches & roads with Howitzer & Field Gun fire from 9 a.m. until 2 p.m. To stop this fire field guns were turned on to known observation stations & gun emplacements with apparent success.

Communication from Divisional Artillery Headquarters with the Headquarters of the Artillery of the 3rd & 28th Divisions was specially arranged for in order that they might co-operate in keeping down hostile gun fire.

Appeals to them met with prompt response & produced it is believed good results, for on the whole the amount & duration of the enemy's gun fire was not as great as previous experience had led me to expect, the MOUND, the principle observing station, on one day in January, having had over 80 large high explosive shell fired at it. During the course of the bombardment, an interesting account of the effect of our 6" Howitzer shell was transmitted by the Artillery Headquarters of the 28th Division, from the observer of a Belgian Battery in action against the enemy's main trench, E.of ST ELOI. All such reports are of value as tending to confirm those received from other sources.

At 5.30 p.m the 3rd Siege Battery ceased fire; the 19th and 20th Brigades soon after increased their rate of fire over the enemy's trenches from opposite Trench No.15 to Trench No. 21.

At 6.p.m the 116th Battery R.G.A. and 61st Battery R.F.A. ceased fire.

The rate of fire was gradually reduced until at 7.45 p.m. a report having been received from the G.O.C. 80th Infantry Brigade that the infantry proceeding to reoccupy the trenches

trenches
no longer required artillery support "Cease fire" was ordered.

During the whole of this day I was in direct telephonic communication with the G.O.C. 80th Infantry Brigade and from about 2.p.m was represented at his Command post by my Staff Captain.

5   All ranks worked well during a long and tiring day.

In this connection I may mention the services of Major. O.R.SWAYNE.R.G.A. 116th Heavy Battery.R.G.A. and of Lieutenant E.J.T.HOUSDEN.R.F.A. 61st Battery R.F.A. who were observing at THE MOUND, a post of considerable danger; without their observations, the practice could not have been carried to its successful conclusion.

6   The forward trench of the enemy was destroyed from the Sap head near trench 22, to a point about the S of SAP in the attached sketch.

7   No.18 round, the first round fired from No.2 gun, fell unfortunately near the MOUND, and fatally wounded a look-out man. It was subsequently found that this Howitzer required at the range of 4100 yards, 1°.40' = 190 yards more elevation than No.1 gun. The difference in elevation based on previous practice at ranges of 2700 to 3000 yards, should have been 30' and to ensure as it was thought, a "plus" round, 20' more had been given, making an allowance of 50' = 100 yards for the first round.

The guns shot alike for line; elevation and line were checked before each round by an Officer.

8.
Ammunition Expended

  18 pdr.   2337.

  4.5" Howitzer 137 Lyddite.

  4.7" Gun 105 Lyddite.

  6" Howitzer 117 Heavy Lyddite.

The effect of the fire of the 4.7" guns and 4.5" Howitzers was satisfactory, the Observing Officers noticing beams etc. blown into the air out of the trenches.

8.3.15.

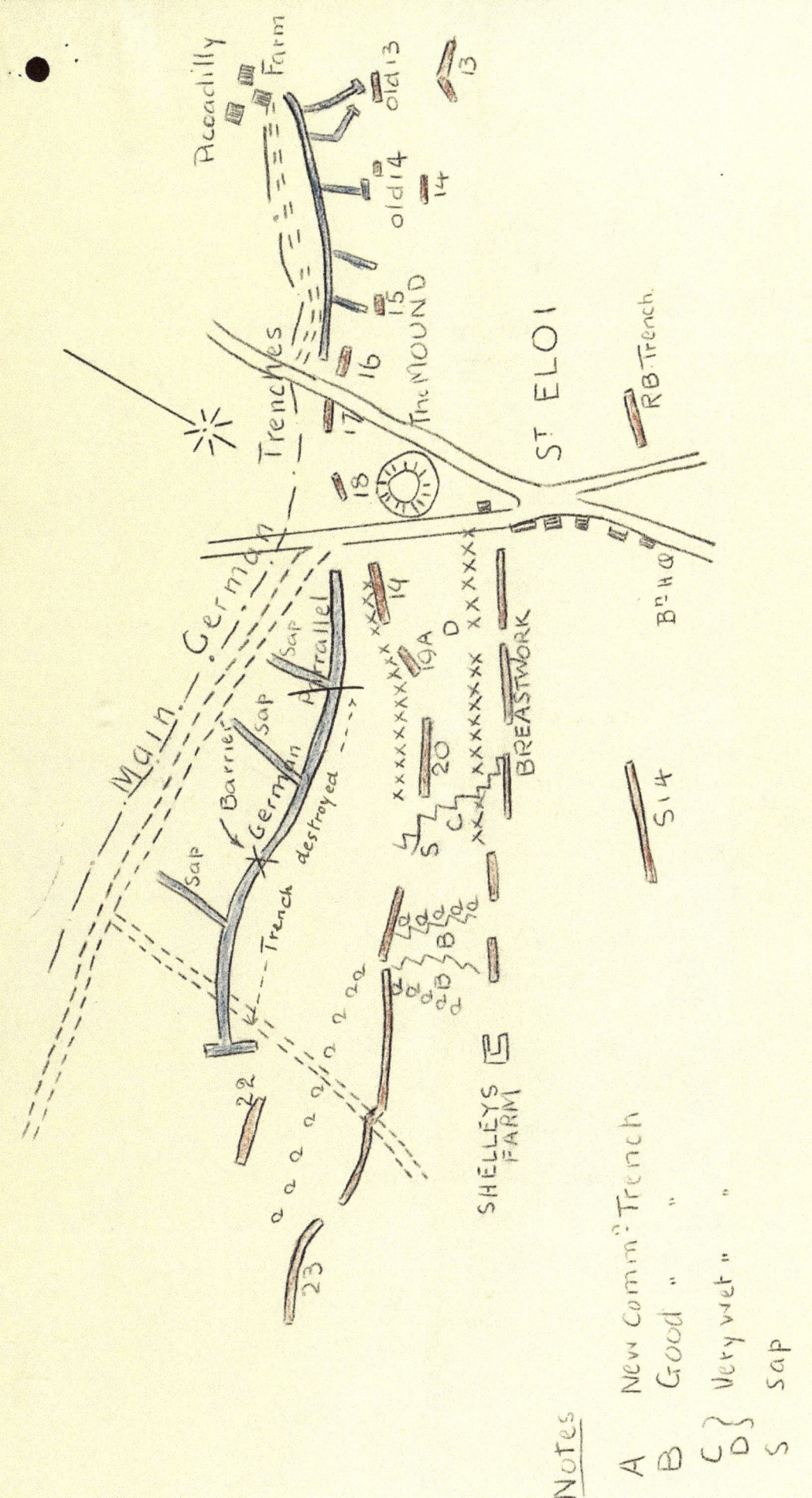

G.O.C. R.A.

G.R. 831.   Sixth.

Reference operation order No.29 of today

1. The G.O.C. R.A. will arrange to open fire directly after dawn 6th inst with 18 pdr shrapnel, on the enemy's trenches in front of our trenches numbers 15, 16, 17, 18.

This fire will continue until the bombardment at 12 noon commences.

It will be of such volume and at such a rate as G.O.C. R.A. considers sufficient to prevent any possibility of enemy occupying the above mentioned trenches which will be evacuated before dawn.

2. This fire is not to commence until G.O.C. Left Section (80th Infy Bde) has reported to G.O.C. R.A. that these trenches are evacuated and clear of our troops. Arrangements must be made by G.O.C. Left Section to ensure rapid transmission of this information to G.O.C. R.A.

3. Acknowledge by wire.

      12.50 a.m. 6-3-15.   (Sd)   H.L.Reed.
                                                        Lt Colonel.G.S.

The fire ordered in para one will be so directed, as long as the enemy makes no movement forward, as to make him still imagine that trenches referred to are still occupied i.e. with safety to imaginary garrisons in their trenches.

                                      (Sd)   H.L.Reed.
                                                 Lt Col.

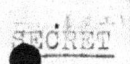

Copy No.

27th Divisional Artillery Operation Order No.3.

Reference Map 1/40,000   March 5th. 1915.

1. The enemy's trenches in O 2 c and d will be attacked by Artillery fire tomorrow.

2. 3rd Siege Battery.
   Commencing at 12 noon the Section 3rd Siege Battery (6" How) will open fire on the enemy's forward trenches opposite our trenches No. 19, 19a, 20 and 21, which as regards 19a and 20 will be evacuated at 11.45 a.m; trench No.19 will be evacuated at dawn, the troops in these being withdrawn to a breastwork in rear. Trench No.21 is not occupied, Trench 22 will remain occupied.

   61st Battery
   At this hour the 61st Battery will open fire on the enemy's forward trenches opposite our Nos. 15, 16, 17, and 18 which will have been evacuated at dawn - Trench No.14 will be in occupation of our troops.

   N.B. Evacuated trenches will be recognisable by reason of white sheets attached to the rear face of the parapet.

   116th Battery.
   At the same hour the 116th Battery will attack the hostile main trench opposite our Nos.15, 16, 17, 18.

3. 3rd Siege Battery.
   When the 3rd Siege Battery has fired approximately 75 rounds its fire will be switched by Order of G.O.C. R.A., to the hostile forward trenches opposite Nos. 15, 16, 17, 18.

   61st Battery.
   At this time the 61st Battery will be ordered by G.O.C. R.A. to attack the enemy's main trench opposite our Nos. 19, 20 and 21.

   116th Battery.
   This Battery will cease fire until the 3rd Siege Battery has ranged, after which it will be ordered by G.O.C. R.A. to re-open fire on its original target.

4. Observation will be as follows :-
   (i) THE MOUND (O 2 d 2.7)
       One observer (61st Battery) for 3rd Siege Battery.
       One observer (116th Battery) for 116th Battery.
   (ii) Breast work in rear of Nos,19, 20 and 21 trenches.
        One observer (20th Bde) for No. 3 Siege Battery.
   (iii) R.B.Trench (O 2 c 8.8)
         One observer (19th Bde) for fire over trenches, No. 15, 16, 17 and 18.
   (iv) BRASSERIE (N 6 a)
        One observer for 61st Battery

5. The O.C. 20th Brigade will arrange to cover the withdrawal of the Infantry garrison of 19a and 20 trenches at 11.45 a.m. by shrapnel fire.

6. The O.C's 19th and 20th Brigades will be prepared to repel any attempt of the enemy to occupy trenches 15, 16, 17, 18, and 19 which are evacuated at dawn.
   The O.C. 1st Brigade will be ready to meet any attempt of the enemy to divert fire from the Left Section where bombardment is taking place.

7. Watches will be adjusted by Signal time.

                                            (sgd) R.H.Hare.
                                                   Lieut:Col.R.A.

Issued at 9.p.m.   Brigade Major, 27th Divisional Artillery.

131/5609

a2
a56

HdQrs R.A. 27th Division

Vol III 1 — 30.4.15

WAR DIARY or **INTELLIGENCE SUMMARY.**

(Erase heading not required.)

Army Form C. 2118.

Hour, Date, Place	Summary of Events and Information	Remarks and references to Appendices
RENINGHELST 1st April 1915	Brigade returns	
2nd " "	The III Heavy Brigade of the Army Artillery is attached to the 5th Corps & is assigned to the 27th Div.	
3rd " "		
4th " "	Head Quarters 27th Div¹ Artillery moved to POTIJZE	
5th " "	Three batteries relieved 1st Brigade RFA relieved the	
6th " "	French: the 4th Battery remained in billets	
7th " "	Two batteries 15th Brigade RFA relieved the French	
7th " "	Two batteries remained in billets	
8th " "	Two batteries of the 20th Brigade relieved the French	
	The Whole of the Battery took up a new position	
	61st Field Howitzer Battery took up a new position in I 12 D	
	The whole of the reliefs were carried out during the nights 6/7 & 7/8 April and was done by Métiers	

19

Army Form C. 2118.

WAR DIARY
or
INTELLIGENCE SUMMARY.
(Erase heading not required.)

Instructions regarding War Diaries and Intelligence Summaries are contained in F.S. Regs., Part II and the Staff Manual respectively. Title pages will be prepared in manuscript.

Hour, Date, Place	Summary of Events and Information	Remarks and references to Appendices
Tuesday April 6th	The 1st, 19th + 20th BDE Ammunition Columns moved Crews billets near VLAMERTINGHE.	
Wednesday April 8th	The Divisional Ammunition column moved to billets East of POPERINGHE. Batteries reported by observation.	
Thursday April 9th	Batteries reported by observation.	
Friday April 10th	All Batteries now in position and Brigades are allotted the following Zones	
	Right Section of line — 20th BDE R.F.A, Nos 1 Bty, with 82nd Infantry BDE	
	Centre Section — 1st BDE R.F.A plus 1 Batty of 20th BDE, with 81st Inf BDE.	
	Left Section — 14th BDE R.F.A with 80th Inf BDE.	
	Batteries reported with aeroplane observation	

WAR DIARY
or
INTELLIGENCE SUMMARY.
(Erase heading not required.)

Army Form C. 2118.

Hour, Date, Place	Summary of Events and Information	Remarks and references to Appendices
POTIJZE		
11th April 1915	Balloon reported into Aeroplane observation	
12th " "	do	
	Major MAIN Commanding 99th Battery R.F.A was wounded in the Infantry Trenches.	
13 " "	Batteries registered	
14th " "	Batteries registered	
15th " "	Batteries registered	
	Batteries reported into wireless aeroplane.	
16th " "	61st Battery shelled a redoubt in Enemys front line. Orders received that no Lyddite is to be fired till further orders.	
	Allotment of ammunition is as follows 3 rounds per gun daily pr 18 Pr.	
	11th Heavy Brigade, 122 + 123 Batteries, one aeroplane under G.O.C.R.A 27th Divn.	

Army Form C. 2118.

WAR DIARY
or
INTELLIGENCE SUMMARY.
(Erase heading not required.)

Instructions regarding War Diaries and Intelligence Summaries are contained in F.S. Regs., Part II and the Staff Manual respectively. Title pages will be prepared in manuscript.

Hour, Date, Place	Summary of Events and Information	Remarks and references to Appendices
17th April	Batteries registered points with Wilson Aeroplane.	Appendix I
7.15pm	Fire from 364 + 99 Batteries took place on roads & approaches on our Extreme right in order to make a demonstration in conjunction with the taking of a trench by the 5th Division on our Right.	27th Division Operation Order No 45
	(a) Rate of fire 30 seconds intervals.	27/17/4/1915
7.20pm	(b) Slow rate of fire	
7.30pm	(c) Rate of fire as in (a) until	
7.35pm	(d) as in (b) until	
7.35pm	(e) as in (a) until	
7.45pm	(f) as in (b) for about 10 minutes.	
7.50pm	(by?)	
7.15pm till	61st Battery + M Btys directed fire into roads about J.31d, J.32.6. and J.22.c.d.	
7.45pm	Slow rate of fire	

Army Form C. 2118.

WAR DIARY
or
INTELLIGENCE SUMMARY.
(Erase heading not required.)

Instructions regarding War Diaries and Intelligence Summaries are contained in F.S. Regs., Part II. and the Staff Manual respectively. Title pages will be prepared in manuscript.

Hour, Date, Place	Summary of Events and Information	Remarks and references to Appendices
18th April 1915.	The name residence was given to the 5th Division at 6.30am.	
19th April	Batteries replied with enemies aeroplane. Enemy's guns were active & fired into YPRES	
20th April 5 am	Assistance was called for by Gen. of 5th Division. Enemy's guns were very active – most batteries were heavily shelled especially the 61st. No casualties. All batteries were turned onto hostile batteries which were dealt with by section by battery, every gun every to have been able.	
	New rate of fire between stops of enemy batteries were located by wireless aeroplane & the information sent to batteries which engaged them	Ref Map 1/20000
6.30	99th Battery was turned on to roads to 135.D and 135.C.1 Ret between 18 and 30 rounds per hour.	
7.40	8 fire Vergnes orders to slacken fire	
8.50	Orders to cease fire	

Army Form C. 2118.

WAR DIARY
or
INTELLIGENCE SUMMARY.
(Erase heading not required.)

Instructions regarding War Diaries and Intelligence Summaries are contained in F. S. Regs., Part II. and the Staff Manual respectively. Title pages will be prepared in manuscript.

Hour, Date, Place	Summary of Events and Information	Remarks and references to Appendices
21st April 1915 6.15PM	5th Division requested assistance. One Battery of 20th BDE was turned on - Rate of fire - bursts of 3 at irregular intervals into slow rate between	which?
7.50 PM	Enemy heavy howitzers shell YPRES. 11th HEAVY BDE turned two batteries on to hostile batteries at J30.13.10.0 and P.1.a	
9 PM	Requested by 5th Division to engage as many of the hostile batteries as possible.	
9.15 PM	Batteries of 20th BDE & 61st Howitzer Battery turned sections onto 9 German gun positions - Bursts of fire roughly every ten minutes	
10 PM 30	11th HEAVY BDE began to engage 14 gun targets - turned bursts of fire on each in turn.	
11.20	Orders received that 4.5" How shells allowance of ammunition must not be exceeded. Order to 61st Battery to Cease Fire.	

24

Army Form C. 2118.

WAR DIARY
or
INTELLIGENCE SUMMARY.
(Erase heading not required.)

Instructions regarding War Diaries and Intelligence Summaries are contained in F.S. Regs., Part II. and the Staff Manual respectively. Title pages will be prepared in manuscript.

Hour, Date, Place	Summary of Events and Information	Remarks and references to Appendices
21st April 2 p.m.	Our H. Battery ordered to cease fire.	
6.40 p.m.	Informed by 5th N. Arty that both Batteries have ceased firing – Order to 26 Bde 'STOP FIRING'.	
22nd April	Seven targets were registered with wireless aeroplane + wireless lamp.	
6.15 Howitzer Battery shelled redoubt opposite French L16 into Apex		
9 pm (about)	Heavy cannonade in NORTH & NORTH WEST.	
	Rumor were received at R.A. H.Qrs	
9½ pm	Orders received to turn as many guns as possible onto direction N – about Squares C.10 & 11.	
	Heavy musketry fire from our trenches in S. point	
23rd April 1.37 A.M.	'R.S.O.S' message received – Firing ordered to cease at 1.45 A.M.	

Army Form C. 2118.

WAR DIARY
or
INTELLIGENCE SUMMARY.
(Erase heading not required.)

Hour, Date, Place	Summary of Events and Information	Remarks and references to Appendices
POTIJZE 23rd April 6.15PM	At request of 5th Division No Battery, 28th Bde was turned onto wood 1.35 - fired 12 rounds consisting of bursts of 3 rounds at irregular intervals.	
7.50	11th Heavy Bde engaged and silenced a hostile Battery in J30.B13	
9 am	Requested by 5th Division to engage as many known hostile Batteries as possible. - This was done.	
10 am	Informed by Artillery Advisor 5th Corps that 4.7 gun ammunition is plentiful.	
10.30am	11th Bde on 14 selected gun targets	
6.40pm	Informed by 5th Div that hostile batteries have ceased firing	
	Expenditure of Ammunition 18 Pr. 9000 (approx) from 23rd – 25th
	4.5" 391
	4.7" 191

Army Form C. 2118.

WAR DIARY
or
INTELLIGENCE SUMMARY.
(Erase heading not required.)

Instructions regarding War Diaries and Intelligence Summaries are contained in F.S. Regs., Part II. and the Staff Manual respectively. Title pages will be prepared in manuscript.

Hour, Date, Place	Summary of Events and Information	Remarks and references to Appendices
24th April 1915 - POTIJZE		
9.30 AM	3 18 Pr Batteries one 4.7 + section 61st Bty turned on to C 12 a + b	
10.45 AM	122 Hy. Bty and Bir how Bty turned onto C11 a + b	
12 midday	1st M.G. + 5th M.G. into X roads in Sq C12 ? 11th H. Bde + 61st Howr onto (cross roads in C6?)	
2.20 p.m.	364th 67 + 148 Batteries turned on the Northern Road	
3.30 p.m.	122 Hy Battery ordered to position in I3 X cross roads running S.W. South + South West from ST JULIEN.	
3.55 p.m.	61st + 26th Bde onto ST JULIEN + road running S.W. + report to 28th Division to withdraw to VLAMETINGHE	
4.30 p.m.	122nd H Batty ordered to ZANDVOORDE + 2 on GHELUVELT	
4.45 p.m.	2 guns 123 H. By. on ZANDVOORDE + 2 on GHELUVELT The above turrets been engaged thro' the buffer tank to Clara note of fire.	

Army Form C. 2118.

WAR DIARY
or
INTELLIGENCE SUMMARY.
(Erase heading not required.)

Hour, Date, Place	Summary of Events and Information	Remarks and references to Appendices
25th April 1915 4.30 AM	Our troops reported to be in S. end of wood in C10+11.	
	All Batteries ordered to neutralize fire to N. of wood & beyond	
9.45 AM	Fire turned onto ground in D13+D14	
9.55 AM	Switched onto D7+8	
10.50 AM	Ordered 61st to STOP Firing	
4.30 PM	Field Batteries onto line drawn thro' C12+D7	
	61st How onto N. of ST JULIEN into Lydddite	
6.45 PM	Rate of fire quickened. 61st How STOP Firing	
7.35 PM	Slow rate of fire.	
7.55 PM	Menin to Ypres evening & heavy rifle fire	
8.40 PM	Slow rate continues through the night.	
	Expenditure Ammunition	
	from 25th — 27th — 18 Pr. 6691	
	4.5 — 191	
	4.7 440	

WAR DIARY
or
INTELLIGENCE SUMMARY.
(Erase heading not required.)

Army Form C. 2118.

Instructions regarding War Diaries and Intelligence Summaries are contained in F.S. Regs., Part II. and the Staff Manual respectively. Title pages will be prepared in manuscript.

Hour, Date, Place	Summary of Events and Information	Remarks and references to Appendices
26th April 1915 POTIJZE 10 AM	Field Batteries turned onto a line between the Crossroads at D7c.0.8 and a point at the S. of Infim. & on bridges Barricades on to house just North of that line	
11 AM	123 Lt. Bty onto heavy guns firing from S.W.	
11.5 AM	Turned 1 gun 61st Howr onto Crossroads at C12.d 10.7	
11.35 AM	" " " " GRAVENSTAFEL Crossroads " " " " GRAVENSTAFEL Ridge & canal road	
	2 Field Batteries onto Ridge GRAVENSTAFEL junction at D16A	Appendix II
11.55 AM	Received 5th Corps Operation Order No 12	5th Corps Operation Order No 12 cl/26/4/15
3 p.m. 3.5 p.m.	113 Batters 149th Bde + 1 Bty 1st Bde onto Zonnebeke Road C10+11 Cancel previous order — Stop firing	
4.5 p.m.	4 Batteries turned on to ridge in D8	
5 p.m.	1st + 119th + 20th Bde ordered to form a "Barrage" of fire North of road in E10+11	
5.15 p.m.	61st Howr on E Crossroads at C11A	
5.20 p.m.	15 cd 61st on C, GC and 1 on C12 & Houses + Crsn Roads	

29

WAR DIARY
or
INTELLIGENCE SUMMARY.
(Erase heading not required.)

Army Form C. 2118.

Instructions regarding War Diaries and Intelligence Summaries are contained in F.S. Regs., Part II and the Staff Manual respectively. Title pages will be prepared in manuscript.

Hour, Date, Place	Summary of Events and Information	Remarks and references to Appendices
26th April 1915 6.8 pm	Orders to Brigade to lengthen their recup.	
27th April 9.17 am	A slow rate of fire was kept up during the night	
	123 H. By directed onto Grn roads in D.9.c.7.9	
	All field Batteries onto ground stretching from cross roads in D.7.c.10.0 to point at Barn D.8.D.10.0 Shrapnel & fire	
12.20 pm	61st By — One Section on S. end of wood in C.10.b.1, and one section in farm at C.17.c	
12.26 pm	20th BDE — One section of guns on road running North from ST JULIEN	
	One section on road from 12 D.	
	One section on road running ST JULIEN N.E. to 12 D.	
1 pm.	3 Batteries into German trenches & farmhouses in C.6.c.7.9 to C.B.7.5.	
2.30 pm.	One section 20th BDE K N. of ST JULIEN.	
3.25 pm.	One section 61st By N. of ST JULIEN	

30

WAR DIARY
or
INTELLIGENCE SUMMARY.
(Erase heading not required.)

Army Form C. 2118.

Instructions regarding War Diaries and Intelligence Summaries are contained in F.S. Regs., Part II and the Staff Manual respectively. Title pages will be prepared in manuscript.

Hour, Date, Place	Summary of Events and Information	Remarks and references to Appendices
27 April 1915 POTIJZE		
4.20 pm	All available guns ordered in C.10, Search Shoout, by C W, heavy winds at a slow rate of fire.	
4.45 pm	2 Horses on farm C.18 B.6.2 and C.16 A5.8. 1 Batty 19 G BDE on x roads N of ST JULIEN	
5.45 pm	Stopped Howitzers	
8.50 pm	Heavy attack on left front (S.E) All batteries opened fire on their zones.	
9 pm	All quiet again - Cease fire.	
10.15 pm	Howitzers on Cross Roads in ST JULIEN. 2 G BDE into Triangle X roads in C.12 - Rate of fire 30 rounds p hour.	
	Ammunition Expenditure 18 p - 2447	
	27th - 28th 4.5 - 140	
	4.7 - 87	

WAR DIARY or INTELLIGENCE SUMMARY

Army Form C. 2118.

Hour, Date, Place	Summary of Events and Information	Remarks and references to Appendices
28. April 15. 1.5 — POTIJZE — 8.45 AM	14th BDE opened fire on ground N. of HANNEBECK Stream between points on western exit of line running N. & S. through F.27 & F.28. Occasionally passed the fire into GERMAN trenches which ran roughly through F.27 & F.28. 6th Howitzers ditto same in 16A & 16B. 2 1/2 Div. Arty forms part of PLUMER'S FORCE.	
1 pm	Artillery ordered to bombard the enemy's trenches on the Northern area as follows. 1st BDE on trenches from C.18.C.4.3 running N.W. C.18.C.10.B.0.10 " " " C.18.C.5.1 to C.18.C.4.3 Bombardment lasted an hour when field guns were turned on to the wood in C.10 different portions being allotted to each Brigade.	
8 pm	Stop firing.	
9 pm	Field Batteries note issued in C.10 & ST JULIEN road & -	

WAR DIARY
or
INTELLIGENCE SUMMARY.
(Erase heading not required.)

Army Form C. 2118.

Hour, Date, Place	Summary of Events and Information	Remarks and references to Appendices
29th April 1915 - POTIJZE	Firing continued throughout the night.	
10.40 PM	Instructions received over the Telephone that the French would attack at midday, the bombardment to commence at 11.30 am and cease at midday.	
11 am	Commenced to BDs. Zones allotted as follows. 1st BDE from farm in C16b thru C16B & 17A, also 1st BDE - from farm in C16b thru C16A & C16B. Sections to road running N-W- 1st BDE on line between farms in C16A to a point running west 20th BDE from farm in C16A to a point running west and includes the Macon N and S through Alt. C. 51st Howitzers in each of the above two zones.	
11.10 am	Germans had the attack of the Mines.	
4 pm	1st BDE instructed to prepare forts around GRAEFENSTAFEL.	
4.45 pm	19th & 20th Bde. on to D.g.c. and D, from there an attack in a S.E. direction.	

Army Form C. 2118.

WAR DIARY
or
INTELLIGENCE SUMMARY.
(Erase heading not required.)

Instructions regarding War Diaries and Intelligence Summaries are contained in F.S. Regs., Part II and the Staff Manual respectively. Title pages will be prepared in manuscript.

Hour, Date, Place	Summary of Events and Information	Remarks and references to Appendices
29th April 1915 (Cont'd) POTIJZE		
4.45 pm	2 Sections 61st on to GRAFENSTAFEL	
5.45 pm	Own fires	
5.50 pm	Batteries turned onto ridge running N.W. and W. from GRAEFSTAFEL between points D9C and D8D0.9	
6.10 pm	1st and 20 BDEs met groups of the enemy's infantry moved in C11D	
7.45	19th BDE on to ST JULIEN through woods.	
	Ammunition expenditure 18pr 2338	
	4.5 111	
	28th – 29th 4.7 27	

Hour, Date, Place	Summary of Events and Information	Remarks and references to Appendices
30th April 1915 – POTIJZE	A slow rate of fire was kept up during the night	
11.10 A.M.	123rd Heavy Battery fired on hostile Battery in J.21.D	
11.45 P.M.	Owing to complaints from our Infantry of 4.7 shells bursting behind their trenches the Battery was stopped firing	
	For the past week the 27th D'V ART'Y have had to deal with two fronts. Enemy targets etc are not entered herein as during the time the attention of the GOCRA & his Staff was drawn to the enemy's main attack from the N. & N.W., at the same time heavy calls were made upon Batteries to support the Infantry whose trenches they covered. The enemy has on many lines pressed successively, he took has been seriously hard interfering not only the actual scene of the firing but on many occasions the shelling of the Town in order to set fire to frean on more keep from serving the person the GOC RA wrote to Staff officer H.Q. Canadians trust in a original memo'm about 10'×12' in tin pounds of POTIJZE CHATEAU which has recently shelled west of the Town.	
	Ammunition Expenditure	18 Pr. 1641
	29-30th	4.5 18
		4.7 34

27th Division

8598/121

Hd Qrs R.A. 27th Division

Part of Vol III

1st to 29th April 1915

Appendix I.

Copy No 8

SECRET.

27th. Division Operation Order No.45.

17th. April, 1915.

1. For reasons communicated verbally to Brigadier Generals R.A. and Infantry Brigades, the following demonstrations with a view to lead the enemy to expect attack by us about the front, trenches 22 to 29, will take place this evening, 17th. instant.

(a) 7-15 p.m. Artillery Fire (20 seconds interval within batteries) by two or three field batteries detailed by G.O.C. R.A. against the enemy's front about opposite our trench 26. - until

(b) 7-20 p.m. Artillery fire slackens and continue slow fire. Infantry detailed by G.O.C. 82nd. and 81st. Infantry Brigades demonstrate with rifle fire on front opposite trenches 22 to 29, until

(c) 7-30 p.m. Infantry slacken fire. Artillery field batteries as in (a) above - until

(d) 7-35 p.m. As in (b) above - until

(e) 7-45 p.m. As in (a) above - until

(f) 7-50 p.m. As in (b) above for about ten minutes when infantry fire will gradually cease.

2. G.O.C. R.A. will arrange for 4.7 guns and 4.5 Howitzers during such periods as he selects (commencing 7-15 p.m.) between 7-15 p.m. and 7-45 p.m. to direct fire on roads about J 31 d. J 32 b. and J 22 c.d.

3. 28th. Division carry out a similar demonstration commencing 7-30 p.m.

4. G.O.C's will issue such instructions as they consider necessary with regard to cessation of work by R.E. and infantry working parties in the vicinity of area of operations.

5. Care to be taken by all concerned to regulate their watches by signal time.

Acknowledge receipt by wire.

Issued at 5-20 pm

Lt. Colonel G.S.
27th Division.

SECRET.   Copy No. 16

5th CORPS OPERATION ORDERS NO. 12.

                                     5th Corps. H.Q.

                                       26/4/15.

1.   The French troops strongly reinforced are attacking the Germans on their front with their right on the YPRES - LANGEMARCK road.

         The LAHORE Div. is to attack this afternoon on the right of the French.

2.   The 5th Corps will co-operate in the attack.

3.   The Lahore Div. is assembling as follows:-
         JULLUNDUR BRIGADE on right and
         FEROZEPORE BRIGADE on left assemble
about WIELTJE and ST JEAN and will be deployed, ready to begin an advance, by 1.20 p.m. from an east and west line from FARM in C. 22. a. to YPRES - LANGEMARCK road.

         The SIRHIND BRIGADE will be in reserve about POTIJZE.

4.   At 1.20 p.m. an artillery bombardment will begin and will be continued till 2.0 p.m. During this time the two brigades of the LAHORE Div. will advance.

         At 2.0 p.m. rapid fire will be begin and continue till 2.5 p.m. when the assault will take place on the German line between the wood in C. 10. d and the YPRES - LANGEMARCK road.

5.   The Canadian Div. will co-operate by pushing forward on the right of the LAHORE DIV. in accordance with special instructions which have been given to mmm. G.O.C. Canadian Divn.

         The 27th and 28th Divs. will engage the enemy

- 2 -

in their front with fire.

6. The artillery of all divisions not required on divisional fronts will co-operate under instructions which have been issued separately.

7. Reports to Chateau in H. 11. a. after 1 p.m.

       H. S. JEUDWINE.

        B.G.G.S.,

         5th Corps.

Issued at 10.30 a.m.

to 27th Div.
  28th Div.
  1st Canadian Div.
  Detachment d'Armee de Belgique.
  Lahore Div.
  Northumbrian Div.
  Cavalry Corps.
  2nd Cavalry Div.

H.d.Q.rs R.A. 27th Division

Vol IV 1 — 31. 5. 15.

12/5/1914

WAR DIARY
or
INTELLIGENCE SUMMARY.

(Erase heading not required.)

Army Form C. 2118.

39

Instructions regarding War Diaries and Intelligence Summaries are contained in F. S. Regs., Part II and the Staff Manual respectively. Title pages will be prepared in manuscript.

Hour, Date, Place	Summary of Events and Information	Remarks and references to Appendices
1st May 1915. # POTIJZE	Batteries fired on enemy's trenches in front of the 2nd Divⁿ Infantry	
	Bde Shelled enemy's redoubt also refer trenches.	
	Results reported to be very satisfactory.	
2.55 p.m.	The following targets were assigned in support of an attack by the LAHORE Division:	
	61st Bde – One section on farm in C16 B 5.2	
	" " " C16 A 5.8	
	14th Bde – One gun from C18 B 5"2 exclusive to bend in road at C16 A 9.5 inclusive	
	1st Bde " from Bend in road inclusive to bin dividing line of C16A and C15C at point 10.0.	
	20th " " " to C15 B 3.8 –	
	Rates of fire 2.50 p.m. to 3 p.m. B.F. 15"	
	3 " 3.15 " 20 "	
	3.15 " 3.30 " 30 "	
	3.30 " 3.15 " St JULIEN	
3.30 p.m.	One gun of 61st Howr directed onto ST JULIEN	
	Three " " " west side of wood in C10	

Army Form C. 2118.

WAR DIARY
or
INTELLIGENCE SUMMARY.
(Erase heading not required.)

Hour, Date, Place	Summary of Events and Information	Remarks and references to Appendices

1st May 1915 – POTIZJE (contd) 3.30 p.m.	1st BDE – 1 Bty on Road Junction at C18 B 4.7 and up the hill for 100ᵡ in a N.W. direction.
	 19 – " and 1 Bty 1st BDE – On W. side of wood in C10.
	 20 – " On centre of hill C10 B.0.0 in S.E. direction.
	
	 Ammunition Expenditure
	 30 April – 1st May 18 Pr. 884
	                        4.5 31
	                        4.7 25	

WAR DIARY or INTELLIGENCE SUMMARY.

Army Form C. 2118.

(Erase heading not required.)

Hour, Date, Place	Summary of Events and Information	Remarks and references to Appendices
2nd May 1915 - POTIJZE	The guns kept up a slow rate of fire during the night and the day on the enemy's trenches on the N. front.	
5.10 p.m.	Enemy attacked from the North bombarding our trenches and the positions in rear - Very heavy. All guns that could fire on that direction were turned on to area C.9, 10 & 11.	
	123rd Heavy Battery left Ypres bec 7.22nd bcfer BREILEN. Ammunition Replenished 18P- 11.57, 4.5-66	
3rd May.	Head Quarters RA moved to farm in H.15A - During the night Artillery Batteries altered to positions as follows.	
	107 BDE 11 H.735 / 12 C.0.2 14 BDE 131 H.B.5 / 15 B.0.9 98 - / 10 D.1.9 39 - / 11 B.8.8 132 " / 9 B.1.0 96 - / 11 C.0.3 133 " / 9 A.5.2 95 - / 9 D.2.4 9th BDE went into billets W. of YPRES.	
	Fairly quiet on the front Ammunition Replenished - 18P- 773 4.5 91	

Army Form C. 2118.

WAR DIARY
or
INTELLIGENCE SUMMARY.
(Erase heading not required.)

Instructions regarding War Diaries and Intelligence Summaries are contained in F.S. Regs., Part II. and the Staff Manual respectively. Title pages will be prepared in manuscript.

Hour, Date, Place	Summary of Events and Information	Remarks and references to Appendices
4th May 1915 - (H15A)	Part of the line was drawn back during the night. The remaining pickets withdrew & new battery positions. 11th Heavy B.E. reported and ordered to take up the following positions during the night. 1 2 2 1 3 D 9 3 1 2 3 1 4 C 1 6 All batteries were heavily shelled during the day. Enemy trenches and places where troops are known to be going on were engaged during the day.	
5th May	Enemy's artillery was very active, most batteries being shelled during the day by field guns and howitzers. The area containing the 5th Artillery is well registered by the enemy and has been for some time past. All ammunition and such work and ammunition has to come through a zone of heavy fire — Ammunition expended 3″ 6″ = 15pr 3436 4.5 1411	

Army Form C. 2118.

WAR DIARY
or
INTELLIGENCE SUMMARY.
(Erase heading not required.)

Hour, Date, Place	Summary of Events and Information	Remarks and references to Appendices
6th May 1915 YPRES (H15A)	No 2 Subsection, 12th Siege Battery (9.2) joined the 2nd Arty and came into position in Sq H10 D 9.4. Batteries reached all approaches, roads & cross roads at intervals during the night. At early dawn they shelled the enemy's trenches for an hour & kept up a slow rate of fire during the day. 4.7 Batteries swept the rover & slopes of WESTHOEK Ridge and pounded the enemy's trenches with good results. 4.7 Batteries reported that the bombardment of the enemy's infantry reported that the enemy's casualties by our trenches reduced their casualties by 50%. 13 in. Bty went into billets West of VLAMERTINGHE, there being out of action and over damaged. 9.6 in. Bty moved to 11 C 0.3. Ammunition Expended 5"/6" 18 Pr. 157 6 4.5 186 - 4.7 385 –	
7th May	Batteries again bombarded enemy's trenches. 9.2 fired on STIRLING CASTLE and from Targets with aerial observation. Spent the same programme Ammunition Expended 7" 6-9 in. 18 Pr. 3930 4.5 620 4.7 815	
8 to 9th		

Army Form C. 2118.

WAR DIARY
or
INTELLIGENCE SUMMARY.
(Erase heading not required.)

Hour, Date, Place	Summary of Events and Information	Remarks and references to Appendices
10th May 1915 – YPRES 7 a.m.	Enemy attacked from the direction of WESTHOEK – ROULERS R[ai]lwy. Violent fighting took place N & S of the division were retained. All guns that could be turned in that direction were retained on – and by their fire especially on the N of the R[ai]lwy (16C) rendered great assistance. Two guns 123 H.By came into position on E of YPRES. Two guns of 114th BDE declared unserviceable by 10 A.M. 98th B[rigad]e withdrawn after attack & replaced by 99th. 364 B[riga]de moved to E 1,13 D 2.3 1, 20 C 4.8 148 H 24 B 9.8 67 Major R. White assumed temporary command of 20th BDE vice Lt-Col P. E. GRAY – sick. Major STEPHENSON three wounded Lt. MILNER killed. All Batteries were under heavy fire west of the Bay. Animals selected 1872 – 1978 4·5 349 4·7 21	

Army Form C. 2118.

WAR DIARY
or
INTELLIGENCE SUMMARY.
(Erase heading not required.)

Hour, Date, Place	Summary of Events and Information	Remarks and references to Appendices
11th July 1915 – YPRES	Batteries engaged enemy's trenches. 9.2 engaged from Targets & Chateau S. of HOOGE. Observation by written aeroplane. Ammunition expended – 18Pr. 3149 – 4.5 500 – 4.7 34.	
12 – "	One Section 5" How – No 4 Bty Durham How Bty came into position at IOD 5.5 leaving two in depot. Batteries keep up slow rate of fire night and day with occasional bursts on enemy's trenches & in places when Infantry were at work. Ammunition expended 18Pr. 657 – 4.5 60 – 4.7 49.	
13 – "	Enemy shelled our Infantry trenches at 6.30am. Cavalry who had replaced our Battalions of the 80th Bde during the night were driven from their front trenches – Batteries opened a barrage of fire and prevented enemy from trooping up reinforcements. Ammunition expended 18Pr. 1295 – 4.5 356.	
14 – "	Very quiet day. Brig Genl UNIACKE Cmdg No 2 GROUP HEAVY ARTILLERY RESERVE took over his 9.2 from + H.A. BDE. Ammunition Expended 18Pr. 280 – 4.5 83.	

Army Form C. 2118.

WAR DIARY
or
INTELLIGENCE SUMMARY.
(Erase heading not required.)

Hour, Date, Place	Summary of Events and Information	Remarks and references to Appendices
15th May 1915 – YPRES	All quiet – Zones reallotted to BDES. Between the dates April 22nd – May 15th, the Div AMM COL sent out 61,423 rounds 18PR Ammunition, 41,832,000 " S.A.A "	
16th " " "	Quiet day – 39th Bty reported 3 rnds	
17th " " "	Section 98th Bty into action at I.8.D.4.2 No aerial observation owing to weather	
18th " " "	1st and 20th BDES a little shooting at enemy's working parties. Bde Major to H.18.D to assist Lt Col EMERY, placed in tactical command of 27 Div ARTY. Bgs Genl STOKES assuming control of 27th & 28th and part of 5D th DIV ARTY under orders of Cavalry Corps Commander.	
19th " "	Remaining section of 98th into action during the night – Quiet on the front – No aerial observation owing to the weather. Major R WHITE killed whilst observing from the trenches.	

Army Form C. 2118.

WAR DIARY
or
INTELLIGENCE SUMMARY.
(Erase heading not required.)

Instructions regarding War Diaries and Intelligence Summaries are contained in F. S. Regs., Part II and the Staff Manual respectively. Title pages will be prepared in manuscript.

Hour, Date, Place	Summary of Events and Information	Remarks and references to Appendices
20 May YPRES	Quiet day – Batteries registered	
21 "	1/3 North 6th 3rd Durham Bty (T) came in – One section I.16.A.2.7, 1/6 A + 6. Section of 4 Durham howitzers engaged in training engaged into last month.	4" North 6th were Hows.
22 "	Front covered by 27 Div MG shortened and 3 mos allotted Bdes as follows – 1st Bde with 3 Durham Bty. From north of BELLE WAARDE Lake to Farm Bd in J.13.c.6.7 to N.W. Corner of wood at J.19.c.4.6. Thence by 19 to Bde to N.W. corner of our line. Thence by 20 to Bde to right of our line.	3rd Durham batts of 3" North Bde were with hows.
23 "	Test practice by following sent to zone just N + S of MENIN Road – 4 Batteries 1st Bde, 1 Bty 4th Northumbrian Bde ×, 4 from 61st How Bde, 1 from 3 Durham How, 1 Bty 19 to Bde. ×	

Army Form C. 2118.

WAR DIARY
or
INTELLIGENCE SUMMARY.
(Erase heading not required.)

Instructions regarding War Diaries and Intelligence Summaries are contained in F.S. Regs., Part II. and the Staff Manual respectively. Title pages will be prepared in manuscript.

Hour, Date, Place	Summary of Events and Information	Remarks and references to Appendices
24th May 1915 - YPRES.	Enemy commenced to attack at about 3 AM., heavy volumes of gas were used in our trenches who those of 4th & 8th Divisions on our left. Batteries opened fire in their Zones and kept up a moderate rate of fire till 8 AM.	
10.20	Information received that enemy had pushed on our back between MENIN ROAD and Railway - a 3 one of artillery fire was established in rear by 1st BDE into LAKE WOOD and DEAD MAN'S BOTTOM - Three Batteries 14th BDE into WOOD running North + South in 112 C and 1813 - Orders given to withdraw 5" How Dublean Bty. Enemy Infantry was held back only by the fire of the field artillery guns - Counter attack by 28th Division made early in the afternoon assisted by fire from 1st BDE and 61st How Bty. Counter attack by 80th Bef. made in early morning	

Army Form C. 2118.

WAR DIARY
or
INTELLIGENCE SUMMARY.
(Erase heading not required.)

Instructions regarding War Diaries and Intelligence Summaries are contained in F.S. Regs., Part II. and the Staff Manual respectively. Title pages will be prepared in manuscript.

Hour, Date, Place	Summary of Events and Information	Remarks and references to Appendices
25th May 1915 YPRES	Quiet day.	
26th " "	20th Bde was relieved by 3rd Northumbrian Bde (T.F.) 15 Pm which began registering.	
27th - 28th "	Northumbrian Bde registered - All quiet.	
29th "	61st How Bty bolted down from Luxtables at HOOGE CHATEAU, on receiving took them on in They bolted. Half Batteries of 1st Bde were relieved by batteries of 3rd Div. and marched south to MENEGATE. 2 sections DIV. Amm. Col. marched to L'Epinette near ARMENTIERES.	
30th " "		
31st " "	Remainder of 1st Bde with half 15th Bde marched to MENEGATE and were relieved by 3rd Div. Hrs. 1 section of Div Amm Col. L'EPINETTE. H.Q. R.A. moved to CROIX DU BAC.	

(73989) W.4141—463. 400,000. 9/14. H.&J.Ltd. Forms/C. 2118/10.

G.B. 571.

G.O.C., Royal Artillery,
   27th Division.

    The Major General Commanding the Division directs me to express to you his admiration at the way the Royal Artillery of the Division has fought and endured day and night during the last 5 weeks.

    The devotion to duty which they have shewn when Batteries have been under appalling and concentrated shell fire in never failing to succour the Infantry when called upon, in unfailing supply of ammunition, in bringing up teams by approaches rendered well nigh impossible by the enemy's guns, is worthy of the great Records of the Royal Artillery.

    The Major General congratulates you and all ranks on their gallant behaviour and himself on having had the honour of including such troops in his Command.

                                              Lieut. Colonel, G.S.,

27th May, 1915.   27th Division.

12/6034

27th Division

H.Q. 2nd R.A. 27th Division
Vol V 1 – 27.6.15.
27th Division

Army Form C. 2118.

WAR DIARY
or
INTELLIGENCE SUMMARY.
(Erase heading not required.)

Hour, Date, Place	Summary of Events and Information	Remarks and references to Appendices
1st June 1915. CROIX DU BAC.	Remainder of 19th BDE received in - The Batteries return then of 6th Divn except the following of the 9th Divn which are attached - 52nd BDE, A, B, C & D Btys. 53rd How Bde, A, B, C & D Btys Also 43rd and 67th How Batteries. The following are positions of Batteries which are grouped under Brigade Commanders - Brig Genl A Stokes. D.S.O. posted to 3rd Corps as Arty adviser - relieved by Brig Genl CAREY. The Artillery groups re-allotted - as under. 12th BDE consisting of 364, 11, 96, & 87 Batteries under Col Dawson to cover front held by 19th Inf BDE 1st BDE consisting of 98, 133, 132 + Composite How BDE - Col Emery to cover front held by 81st Inf BDE. 25th BDE consisting of 99, 148, 67 & 43 Batteries under Col WAY to cover front held by 80th Inf BDE 14th BDE consisting of 39, 96, 131, + 4 How Batteries under Col SMYTHE to cover front held by 82 Inf BDE.	See Appendix marked A.
5th June		

WAR DIARY
or
INTELLIGENCE SUMMARY.
(Erase heading not required.)

Army Form C. 2118.

Hour, Date, Place	Summary of Events and Information	Remarks and references to Appendices
6th June 1918. Croix du Bac	Batteries registered new zones. Positions of batteries as shown in Appendix II	
7th "	52nd BDE rejoined 9th Div.	
"	62nd BDE (12th Div") marched in to wagon lines	
8 "	62nd BDE - Batteries went into position near abbatoir	
"	Heath group - Appendix II	
9th "	Registration - little shelling by enemy	
10th "	65th How BDE, 12th Div" marched in - A B4 went into position after 8 pm - Appendix II	
"	43rd, 87th How Batteries withdrawn to wagon lines and were replaced by A/65 and A/53 respectively.	
13 } 14 }	53rd BDE marched South to rejoin 9th Division less A/53	

Army Form C. 2118.

WAR DIARY
or
INTELLIGENCE SUMMARY.
(Erase heading not required.)

Instructions regarding War Diaries and Intelligence Summaries are contained in F.S. Regs., Part II and the Staff Manual respectively. Title pages will be prepared in manuscript.

Hour, Date, Place	Summary of Events and Information	Remarks and references to Appendices
15th June 1915 ARMENTIERES	12th Brigade relieved North & join the 6th Division — Major D.M. Harris took over command of the 12th BDE. group of Batteries — This group named "A" Group.	
18th " "	131st and 4th Warwick How Batteries joined in place where two of our ammo boxes exploded at C.17.A.3.5. Results were food and ammo dets disposed in very rough over in a wood to the rear	
25th " "	62nd BDE, 12th Division, relieved from our Division	
27th " "	65th BDE, less C/Battery relieved by 72nd Division	

APPENDIX I

53nd Brigade.R.F.A. Col. KNAPP.

  "A"Bty. H 23 B 1.2.
  "B" .. H 24 C 6.1.
  "C" .. H 23 A 1.1.
  "D" .. H 18 B 5.5.
  95th.. H 24 C 3.8. Attached
  131st.. H 24 C 1.5. "
  39th.. I 13 C 2.6. "

12th Brigade.R.F.A. Col. DAVSON.

  87th.. I 19 A 8.7.
  C/52nd I 7 B 5.5. Attached
  96th.. I 13 A 8.8. "

1st Brigade.R.F.A. Col. EMERY.

  11th.. H 24 C 3.9.
  98th.. I 7 B 5.5.
  132nd.. I 8 B 3.5.
  133rd.. I 9 A 9.8.

Composite Howr Bty consisting of
 1 Section 43rd and 1 Section
 87th Bty at I 8 A 4.6.

20th Brigade.R.F.A. Col. KAY.

  67th.. C 26 C 5.2.
  99th.. C 27 D 0.6.
  148th.. C 27 B 0.0.
  364th.. In Wagon Line.
  43rd.. C 27 A 10.7. Attached

APPENDIX II

12th Brigade.R.F.A.   Lt.Col.DAVSON.   "A" group

    11th Bty.   H 24 C 3.9.
    96th   ..   L 13 B 2.9.
    364th ..   H 24 C 1.7.
    87th   ..   I 19 A 7.9.
    A/62nd ..   H 23 B 1.2.
    D/65th ..   H 18 B 6.6.

1st Brigade.R.F.A.   Lt.Col.EMERY.   "B" group

    98th Bty.   I 13 B 2.8.
    132nd ..   I 8 B 3.5.
    133rd ..   I 9 A 9.9.
    B/62nd ..   I 9 A 9.9.
    C/65th ..   I 9 C 3.9.

20th Brigade.R.F.A.   Lt.Col.KAY.   "C" group

    67th Bty.   C 26 D 8.1.
    99th   ..   C 27 D 2.8.
    148th ..   C 27 B 2.4.
    C/62nd ..   C 20 D 5.4.
    B/65th ..   C 27 A 1.8.
    43rd   ..   C 27 A 8.6.

19th Brigade.R.F.A.   Lt.Col.SMYTH.   "D" group

    95th Bty.   C 7 A 5.5.
    131st   ..   C 19 B 5.7.
    39th   ..   C 14 B 3.8.
    Warwick Howr. C 21 C 1.8.
    D/62nd ..   C 19 B 5.8.
    A/65th ..   C 28 A 1.8.

1080/12/

27th Division

HdQrs R.A. 27th Division

Not 41

July 15.

WAR DIARY
or
INTELLIGENCE SUMMARY.
(Erase heading not required.)

Army Form C. 2118.

Hour, Date, Place	Summary of Events and Information	Remarks and references to Appendices
CROIX-du-BAC night 15/16 July	Front occupied by 82nd Infantry Brigade was taken over by the 12th Division.	
" 16/17 "	Sections of 19th Bde R.F.A were relieved by sections of 12th Div. Artillery. Part of 80th Bde front was taken over by the 58th Div. Sections of 20th Bde R.F.A were relieved by sections of 58th Div. Artillery.	
17/18	Front of Division was occupied by 1st and 19th Infantry Brigades covered by "A" & "B" Artillery groups. A group consists of 19th Bde RFA with two Batteries 20th Bde and A/53 Howitzer Battery. B group consists of 1st Bde RFA with 2 Batteries 20th Bde and B/65 Howitzer Battery.	

Army Form C. 2118.

WAR DIARY
or
INTELLIGENCE SUMMARY.
(Erase heading not required.)

Hour, Date, Place	Summary of Events and Information	Remarks and references to Appendices
CROIX - du - BAC 18/19 July	Relief of Batteries completed.	
21st "	Permission given for limited ammunition to be expended if a suitable target presents itself.	
31st "	The Batteries of "B" Group with 3.7", 14.8" & A/53 How Batteries of "A" group and two howitzer guns carried out a bombardment of the hostile redoubt opposite trenches 59, 60, 61 and 62. Operation order by O.C. "B" group attached. The amount of ammunition allowed was not sufficient to test its own effectiveness. The German reply was very feeble and ineffective bombs being severely directed.	Appendix 1 Operation order by O.C. "B" group.

27th Division

D1/6971

Hd Qrs R.A. 27th Division

Vol VII

August & Sept. 15

WAR DIARY
OR
INTELLIGENCE SUMMARY.
(Erase heading not required.)

Army Form C. 2118.

Instructions regarding War Diaries and Intelligence Summaries are contained in F.S. Regs., Part II. and the Staff Manual respectively. Title pages will be prepared in manuscript.

Hour, Date, Place	Summary of Events and Information	Remarks and references to Appendices
Croix du BAC 2nd August 1915	O.C. & Hd Quarters of F.A. Bde with 4 Battery commanders & 4 sergeants from 20th Division arrived & are attached to "A" Bty for 3 days.	
7 hr	O.C. & Hd Quarters of F.A. Bde (4.5" Hows) with 2 Battery commanders, 2 Subalterns & 2 Sergeants arrived & are attached to "B" Bty for 3 days.	
10 hr	Two Battery commanders, 2 Subalterns & 2 Sergeants arrived & are attached to the Howitzer Batteries for 3 days. A/92 How Battery (4.5") came into this Div" from the 20th Division 20 hrs to make up the establishment of Hows to 12 guns. The Battery went to its wagon lines pending the completion of its sub-position.	

Army Form C. 2118.

WAR DIARY
or
INTELLIGENCE SUMMARY.
(Erase heading not required.)

Hour, Date, Place	Summary of Events and Information	Remarks and references to Appendices
Croix-du-Bac 28th August 1915	A/92 Howitzer Battery began registering from junction at H18C9.4.	
29th August 1915	Lieut M.O.M. Wynne was killed by a stray shell when walking in ARMENTIERES.	

Army Form C. 2118.

WAR DIARY or INTELLIGENCE SUMMARY.
(Erase heading not required.)

Hour, Date, Place	Summary of Events and Information	Remarks and references to Appendices
CROIX-du-BAC September	Orders to forthcoming operations by 8th Division accompanied are made for regrouping of the Artillery - Regrouping group to consist of the following Batteries:- 11th, 364, 96b, 146b, 34th, 131st, 95th + 33rd (from 8 Div) in exchange for bie 67th (T.&M.D Div) 129 bde begin Evan - consisting of 'A', 'B' & 'C' Batteries. All Batteries except the following remain in their present positions. C/129 H29 B 1.5 / 11 H24 A 2.4 / 364 H24 A 6.8 / 148 H24 B 8.8 / 96 119 A 1.2	
8th -	Completion of moves to new positions which had been prepared during the previous week completed except a section each of 11th & 364 & Bdys which remain in old positions to cover 27 In Bn front.	

WAR DIARY
or
INTELLIGENCE SUMMARY.
(Erase heading not required.)

Army Form C. 2118.

Hour, Date, Place	Summary of Events and Information	Remarks and references to Appendices

Croix du BAC September 9th (cont'd)	Seven batteries, 4 18Pr and 3 4.5" Howitzers, were formed of another F.A. Bde. of the 23rd Division came into the 27th Divn area at MENEGATE. Sections of the following came into positions as follows during night 8/9th.
	
	102nd Bde R.F.A. — Lt Colonel Biddulph
	   "B" Battery H.18.B.6.8 in A Group
	   "C" " I.8.D.0.3 " " "
	104th Bde. R.F.A. → Colonel E.A. Hobson
	   "B" " I.13.B.1.9 " B "
	   "D" " I.13.C.4.5 " " "
	105th How. Bde R.F.A. — Lt Colonel W.A. Nicholson
	   A " I.7.B.4.5 " B "
	   B " I.8.A.7.5 " " "
	   D " I.13.B.2.9 " A "	

WAR DIARY
or
INTELLIGENCE SUMMARY.
(Erase heading not required.)

Army Form C. 2118.

Hour, Date, Place	Summary of Events and Information	Remarks and references to Appendices
CROIX du BAC September 9th	The remaining returns of the attached batteries went into position night 9/10th.	
	BRIG: GENERAL H.D. WHITE-THOMSON, C.B, D.S.O. Arrived from the Cavalry Corps to take over C.R.A. of the Division vice Brig: Genl. G.G.S. CAREY to 11th Corps.	
September 11th	Orders received that the 27th Division will be relieved by the 23rd Division by the night 16/17th.	
12th	The following relief took place evening of 11th. Section of 125th Bde by section of 105th Bde A/103 Bty " " 96th " " " B/103 " " " 364 " " " C/103 " " " 148 " " "	
13th	The following reliefs took place on night 12/13 Section 11th Bty by section 96th B/102 " 132 " " " A/103 " 96 " " " 1st M5 " 67	

Army Form C. 2118.

WAR DIARY
or
INTELLIGENCE SUMMARY.
(Erase heading not required.)

Hour, Date, Place	Summary of Events and Information	Remarks and references to Appendices
CROIX DU BAC 13th September 1915	Section 1st Battery by section D/103	
12 -	" 9/4" " " C/104	
	A gun of the 133rd Battery burst whilst firing H.E. experimental ammunition - there were no casualties. The experimental fuses with H.E. was extraordinary	
13th September	A shell burst in the bore of gun of 364 Battery but did not detonate & only bulged the piece. No casualties	
10.30 am	New billetting area occupied - near MERRIS.	
11 am	From at position of 99th Bty was shelled by 4.2" Hows + out of fire - About 40 rounds fell - No casualties.	
	The enemy shelled ARMENTIERES during the day with 4.2"	

WAR DIARY or INTELLIGENCE SUMMARY.

Army Form C. 2118.

Hour, Date, Place	Summary of Events and Information	Remarks and references to Appendices
CROIX DU BAC 14th September	The Divl. Amm Col and AMM Cols of the 1st & 2nd Bdes marched back to MERRIS area - Corresponding AMM Cols 23rd Division replaced them.	
15.40 "	The remaining returns of all batteries except those of 23rd & 19th Bde which remain attached to the 23rd Division were relieved during night 14/15th.	
10 am "	1st, 20th & 124th Bdes marched to the new billeting area near MERRIS.	
16th "	C.R.A. 27th Division handed over command to C.R.A. 23rd Division at 10 am. R.A. Head Quarters marched to Billets at MERRIS. Information received that 19th Bde R.F.A. will rejoin the Division, marching to new billeting area night 16/17th.	

WAR DIARY
or
INTELLIGENCE SUMMARY.

(Erase heading not required.)

Army Form C. 2118.

Hour, Date, Place	Summary of Events and Information	Remarks and references to Appendices
MERRIS. 17th September.	All Brigades route marched. B.G. R.A. left by motor for AMIENS.	
18th, 19th, 20th & 21st.	The Division entrained + were moved to stations west of AMIENS. The 1st Bde entrained at LONGEAU went into position on nights 19/20th, 20/21st, relieving the French Artillery. The Division remained in temporary billets at WARFUSÉE - ABANCOURT during 20th moving to MERICOURT on the 21st.	

WAR DIARY or INTELLIGENCE SUMMARY

Army Form C. 2118.

Hour, Date, Place	Summary of Events and Information	Remarks and references to Appendices
MERICOURT 22nd September	Sections of "B" and "E" Batteries 129th Bde moved into position. 14th Bde moved up to their wagon lines. Emplacements for 39, 95 & 96 Batteries were commenced.	
23rd	Operations as shown in attached programme were carried out. Enemy's shelling. 15 rounds from 5.9 inch fell close to 14th Bde. Three salvos of 4 rounds from a 77mm fell 250 yards over 133 Bty. 2nd Canadian Bty (Major Scully) marched into the 27 Brit. Area.	Appendix I
24th	One section 39th Bty joined the 98th – forming a 6 gun Bty. 95th, 96th & remaining sections 39th took-hole position during night 23rd/24th.	

(73989) W4141—463. 400,000. 9/14. H.&J.Ltd. Forms/C. 2118/10.

Army Form C. 2118.

WAR DIARY
or
INTELLIGENCE SUMMARY.
(Erase heading not required.)

Instructions regarding War Diaries and Intelligence Summaries are contained in F. S. Regs., Part II. and the Staff Manual respectively. Title pages will be prepared in manuscript.

Hour, Date, Place	Summary of Events and Information	Remarks and references to Appendices
MERICOURT – 24th Sept.	Operations as shown on the attached programme were carried out.	Appendix II.
25th "	67 and 364 Batteries went into position night 24th/25th. 2nd Canadian Heavy Battery marched in and encamped at PROYART.	
26th "	Operations as detailed in the attached programme were carried out. 97th & 384th Batteries have withdrawn during tonight to the 2.0. Wagon Lines. Very little shelling in retaliation by the enemy	Appendix III.
9.15 p.m.	98th Bty fired on line cut through wire where enemy were attempting to repair it	
27th.	Orders received to commence evacuation – limited to defensive action only – One section 148 Hy Battery relieved by section 131 S/Bty	

(73989) W4141–463. 400,000. 9/14. H.&J.Ltd. Forms/C. 2118/10.

Army Form C. 2118.

WAR DIARY
or
INTELLIGENCE SUMMARY.
(Erase heading not required.)

Instructions regarding War Diaries and Intelligence Summaries are contained in F.S. Regs., Part II. and the Staff Manual respectively. Title pages will be prepared in manuscript.

Hour, Date, Place	Summary of Events and Information	Remarks and references to Appendices
MORICOURT September 28th	Second Section 148th MG relieved by Section 131st BG	
29th	Quiet day. Enemy's activity was chiefly confined to the employment of minenwerfers onto our front trenches. Enemy fired a few rounds of 7.7 mm during day. Our 4.5 Howitzer was occupied in taking in trench minenwerfers — 2nd Cavalier H.Battery (47) fired 6 rounds of shrapnel [?] into Birken Aeroplane.	
30th	Quiet day.	

SECRET.

Appendix I 7'

27th Divisional Artillery.

PROGRAMME OF OPERATIONS.

1st Day.

UNIT.	OBJECTIVE.	TIME.	No. of rounds per battery.	Total No. of rounds.	Remarks.
133rd Bty.) 132nd ") 98th ") 11th ")	ENEMY'S FRONT LINE TRENCHES.	3 - 3.30 p.m. 5 - 5.30 p.m.	120 SHRAPNEL. 20 H.E.	480 80.	
1 Sect.B/129 Bde.	Register points from 518 to 535.	During day.	50.	50.	
1 Sect.C/129 Bde.	Register and fire on MINE SHAFT 200 yards North of 1 in Pt.541.	During day.	50.	50.	

SECRET. 27th Divisional Artillery.

Appendix II 72

2nd Day.

PROGRAMME OF OPERATIONS

UNIT.	OBJECTIVE.	TIME.	No. of rounds per Battery.	Total No. of rounds.
133rd Bty.) 132nd ")	Enemy's front line trenches.	2.30 – 3.p.m. & 4.30 – 5.p.m	10 H.E. 60 Shrapnel.	70. 70.
98th plus ½ of 39th Bty.	Wire, trenches 515 to 518.	2.30 – 3.p.m & 4.30 – 5.p.m.	25 H.E. 100 Shrapnel.	125.
11th Bty.	Enemy's front line trenches.	2.30 – 3.p.m. & 4.30 – 5.p.m.	15 H.E. 63 Shrapnel.	78.
Sect. 39th Bty.	DOMPIERRE Trenches from the road to Pt.541.	2.30 – 3.p.m & 4.30 – 5.p.m.	30 Shrapnel.	
96th Bty.	Trenches 538 to 541.	2.30 – 3.p.m & 4.30 – 5.p.m	10 H.E. 50 Shrapnel.	60.
95th Bty.	Trenches 541 to road junction.	2.30 – 3.p.m. & 4.30 – 5.p.m	10 H.E. 50 Shrapnel.	60.
1 Sect.C/129 Bde.	Register and fire on points MINE SHAFT 200 yards North of 1 in Pt.541.	2.30 – 3.p.m & 4.30 – 5.p.m.	50 per Section.	
1 Sect. B/129 Bde.	Trenches 529 – 535.	2.30 – 3.p.m. & 4.30 – 5.p.m.	50 per Section.	

SECRET.

Appendix II

27th Divisional Artillery.

3rd Day.

PROGRAMME OF OPERATIONS.

unit.	objective.	No. of rounds.	Time.	Total No. of rounds.
133rd Bty.) 132nd ")	Distribute their fire along the trenches of their original points.	15 H.E. 60 Shrapnel.	Simultaneous fire will be opened at 2 - 2.30 p.m. and 4 - 4.30 p.m.	150.
98th plus ½ of 39th Bty.	Concentrate fire on wire and trenches at BOIS TRIANGULAIRE and 200 yards N.E. of it.	30 H.E. 100 Shrapnel.		130.
11th Bty.	Front trenches from Pt.541 to road junction E. of DOMPIERRE.	20 H.E. 60 Shrapnel.		80.
96th Bty.	Front trenches from Pt.538 to Pt.541.	20 H.E. 60 Shrapnel.		80.
Sect.39th Bty.	Enfilade DOMPIERRE Trenches from road fork to Pt.541.	40 Shrapnel.		40.
95th Bty.	Register zone between cross roads 800 yards W. of D in DOMPIERRE and Pt.564.	Up to 40 Shrapnel.	During day.	40.
Sections B & C Batteries 129th Bde.	LOCATED MINENWERFERS.	Not to exceed 50 rounds per section.		50.
67th Bty.	Wire Cutting.	400 Shrapnel.	2 - 2.30 p.m.	400
364th Bty.	Wire Cutting.	400 Shrapnel.	4.45-5.15 p.m	400

74

12/74·35

CRA.
C.R.A. 27th Divn.

Dec '15

Vol IX VIII

WAR DIARY
or
INTELLIGENCE SUMMARY.
(Erase heading not required.)

Army Form C. 2118.

Hour, Date, Place	Summary of Events and Information	Remarks and references to Appendices
MERICOURT – October 1st.	Orders received for attachment of 2 Batteries 18Pr and 2 Batteries 4.5" Howitzers to the 27th Div. Artillery from the 2nd instant for training purposes. Quiet day – About 20 4.2 Shells fell in the Batt. Area and a few rounds of 77 mm.	
" 2nd	Quiet day – 2 Batteries 114th Bde and 2 Batteries 117th Hows Bde of the 26th Division marched in – Sections of each of the latter relieved sections of 'B' & 'C' 129 during the night. The 18Prs went into position in proximity to the Batteries of 125 Bde. Ammunition for attached Batteries limited to 50 rounds 18Pr per Batt. and 20 rounds per How. (4.5).	
" 3rd	Rather more Shelling than usual by hostile guns.	
" 4th	Canadian Heavy Battery registered a few points.	
" 5th	Enemy's 4.2 Howitzer and 77mm Batteries fired about 50 rounds on our front trenches during the day	
" 6th	Enemy gun was in new action – 70680. 4.2 Hows Shells being directed into H.Q. A & S. Highlanders.	

WAR DIARY
or
INTELLIGENCE SUMMARY.
(Erase heading not required.)

Army Form C. 2118.

Hour, Date, Place	Summary of Events and Information	Remarks and references to Appendices
MERICOURT - 6th October. (Contd)	Sections of each Battery 19th Bde were relieved by sections of Batteries 20th Bde.	
7th "	The hostile guns were more active especially in front of DOMPIERRE. 77 mm & 4.2 Hows fired.	
	The relief of the 19th Bde Brigade was completed during the night. Observation was difficult before 10 am owing to the haze. Hostile guns were more in less active against our front Batteries: chiefly 77 mm & 4.2 howitzers.	
8th "	Enemy's guns not so busy. HINDENBEATER which fired into O 3 Trench was silenced by our 4.5 Hows.	
9th "	The attached Batteries of 26th Div. viz A + B 117 How Bde A + B 114 Bde and B + C 6 Bde against their own were replaced by the own Brigades -	

WAR DIARY
or
INTELLIGENCE SUMMARY.
(Erase heading not required.)

Army Form C. 2118.

Hour, Date, Place	Summary of Events and Information	Remarks and references to Appendices
MERICOURT - 10th October	Owing to the mist observation was difficult. 3 or 4 MINENWERFERS opened fire on L and K2 trenches. 132nd Battery replied round for round.	
11th "	Some experience with Planes. Some 50 rounds were fired in retaliation to hostile fire. Fairly quiet day.	
12th "	No hostile shells fell in the area during the 24 hours.	
13th "	About 60 77 mm shells were fired by the enemy. And about 42 4.2 Hows. Three Trench Mortars and Minenwerfers were also active. The 27th Siege How Section fired 30 rounds and 18 Prs retaliated on hostile trenches.	
14th "	Enemy's Artillery was somewhat more active than in the previous day. Enemy about 160 rounds from 77 mm guns and 4.2 Hows. Six guns fired 120 rounds chiefly retaliation and registration.	

WAR DIARY
or
INTELLIGENCE SUMMARY.
(Erase heading not required.)

Army Form C. 2118.

Hour, Date, Place	Summary of Events and Information	Remarks and references to Appendices
MERICOURT - 15th October	Hostile artillery and one own guns, rifles also had all day and observation of ground behind the enemys trenches impossible.	
" 16th "	Relatively quiet day. Attached batteries 26th Bde, viz C+D 114th Bde arrd C + D 117 "Bde" left for the 5th Division.	
" 17th "	Owing to mist nothing could be observed in rear of the enemys trenches.	
" 18th "	Normal day	
" 19th "	Hostile aeroplanes very active.	
" 20th "	Very quiet day - not a single round was fired from enemys guns.	

Army Form C. 2118.

WAR DIARY
or
INTELLIGENCE SUMMARY.
(Erase heading not required.)

Hour, Date, Place	Summary of Events and Information	Remarks and references to Appendices
MERICOURT 21st October	Our Troops retired by the enemy.	
22nd "	G.O.C. Division inspected 19th Bde, 20th Bde and 1st Bde Ammunition Columns also A/13, B/5 at CERISY.	
23rd "	Quiet day. Part of 20th Bde withdrawn	
24th "	Remainder of 20th Bde withdrawn	
	1st Bde relieved by sections of 6th Div: (French) on right 24th/25th.	
25th "	The remainder of the 1st Bde relieved by the French.	
26th "	The whole of the Div: Artillery now in rest billets west of AMIENS.	

121/7637

H. Q. R.A. 27th Dn.

Nov 1915

Vol IX

Army Form C. 2118.

WAR DIARY
or
INTELLIGENCE SUMMARY.

(Erase heading not required.)

Instructions regarding War Diaries and Intelligence Summaries are contained in F.S. Regs., Part II. and the Staff Manual respectively. Title pages will be prepared in manuscript.

Hour, Date, Place	Summary of Events and Information	Remarks and references to Appendices
GUINEMICOURT — November		
21st	The Divisional Artillery remained in rest billets during the rest of the month - Battery and Brigade training was carried out during that time. Lt. Colonel EMERY, C.M.G. took over command vice Brig. Genl. WHITE-THOMSON, C.B. D.S.O. invalided home, on account of an accident.	

www.ingramcontent.com/pod-product-compliance
Lightning Source LLC
Chambersburg PA
CBHW081545160426
43191CB00011B/1848